# *Writing for Children*

# Writing for Children

by

Catherine Woolley

(who is also Jane Thayer)

NAL BOOKS

NEW AMERICAN LIBRARY

A DIVISION OF PENGUIN BOOKS USA INC., NEW YORK

PUBLISHED IN CANADA BY

PENGUIN BOOKS CANADA LIMITED, MARKHAM, ONTARIO

Published simultaneously in Canada by Penguin Books Canada Limited

NAL TRADEMARK REG. U.S. PAT. OFF. AND FOREIGN COUNTRIES
REGISTERED TRADEMARK—MARCA REGISTRADA
HECHO EN DRESDEN, TN, U.S.A.

SIGNET, SIGNET CLASSIC, MENTOR, ONYX, PLUME, MERIDIAN and NAL BOOKS are published *in the United States* by New American Library, a division of Penguin Books USA Inc., 1633 Broadway, New York, New York 10019, *in Canada* by Penguin Books Canada Limited, 2801 John Street, Markham, Ontario L3R 1B4

Library of Congress Cataloging-in-Publication Data

Woolley, Catherine.
Writing for children / by Catherine Woolley.
p. cm.
ISBN 0-453-00707-4
1. Children's literature—Authorship. I. Title.
PN147.5.W6 1990
808.06′8—dc20 89-36908
CIP

First Printing, January, 1990

1 2 3 4 5 6 7 8 9

PRINTED IN THE UNITED STATES OF AMERICA

TO
all the people
who have asked my help
in writing a book
and
the people whose
experience and counsel
helped me in the writing
of this book

# Contents

# *Introduction*

In late 1983 I discovered that a Japanese friend had a gift for words. But Yoko Kawashima Watkins, although fluent in speaking and comprehending English perfectly, had no grasp of English grammar or of how to structure raw material into a novel. Here was a talent not to be wasted, and I invited Yoko to meet with me once a week. I had conducted workshops in juvenile writing and I had my notes.

Almost with anguish, Yoko decided that with this support she could write a story that had haunted her for forty years—the story of her escape from North Korea at the end of World War II. I became teacher, then editor. The result was *So Far From the Bamboo Grove,* a teenage novel published in 1986 that took top awards.

Yoko taped our conversations and several professional and would-be professional writers listened to the tapes, took notes, and said, "You ought to write a book about writing for children." "I don't want to," I said. "It's your duty to write a book!" "Oh well. Maybe. Sometime."

I sat in my garden and thought about it. I had done my life's work, eighty-seven books for children recorded in *Who's Who in America.* I was enrolled in the New Jersey literary Hall of Fame. Some books, published more than forty years ago, were beginning a new life in paperback. My stories were included in anthologies, school readers and teachers' manuals, and some had been translated into Japanese. Never again would I need to pound a typewriter.

Then I thought of all the hopeful writers who had sent me

manuscripts, asking advice. It was frustrating not to be able to pass on all I wanted to tell them about writing for children. Well, maybe . . .

The more I thought about it, the more I wanted to write about writing for childern. I wrote this book.

—*Catherine Woolley*

# 1

# *Is Writing for Children Easy?*

I'm going to plunge you straight into the creative process. That's what you're interested in, and you're impatient to get going. I'll tell you how three pieces of my writing were born.

Some years ago, the Woodstock rock festival turned into a jumble—bedlam, refuse, hungry and sometimes sick young people, and an unbelievable traffic jam. I was fascinated and kept every newspaper clipping. Then I moved a fictional crowd of teenagers, stranded for the night before they reached the festival in their broken-down cars and unsuitable walking shoes, onto the lawn of a house I had used in another book. I wrote *Cathy and the Beautiful People*.

A very different birthplace for a story was a small-town school at three P.M. I saw the local taxi man, with responsibility for transporting several small boys and girls, collect his charges by shouting, "I bet I can beat you to the car!" They got there first. Amused, I wrote a story, *Mike the Taxi Man,* for a juvenile magazine.

The third example is my book *Ginnie and Geneva,* which started with the very different personalities of me and my best friend in fourth grade.

If some event interests you most, the action in a book will grow out of the event. If a child intrigues you, you develop a story that grows out of the child's nature. Given the character's traits and tendencies, you ask yourself, what will happen if you place him or her in a given situation? In either case the story you develop is the meat of your book. It is known as the *conflict.*

Now put part of your mind to work cogitating on this creative process. We'll get to the details of conflict and all the other juvenile writing techniques in later chapters. The other part of your mind must be contemplating some qualities and aptitudes necessary to the beginning writer.

I had asked three young friends to come for a cup of tea or something, and we sat in the parlor in my little old house in Truro on Cape Cod and talked. One of my guests was a teacher in a prestigious preparatory school. His wife had taught fourth grade in a private school. The third was a supervisor of English in a city in Massachusetts and buys the books for kindergarten through grade twelve. They had come partly because they had been bidden, partly because they love books and love to talk about books. I told them I was hoping to write a book about writing for children and needed their advice.

Their interest lay in establishing reading habits in children that will go on for a lifetime. They knew a lot about books. They knew that children of all ages love fantasy and they cited *The Lion, the Witch and the Wardrobe* and *The Magician's Nephew* by C. S. Lewis. They knew tenth-graders will not read Charles Dickens on their own, but enjoy Dickens if he is presented by a good teacher. Children are "crazy" about *The Call of the Wild* by Jack London.

They did not mind a little mild profanity or sex in a child's book, but yes, they said, the people who made up book lists had to be cautious. These educators were much more interested in the values in books, so that children would not grow up believing the only important things were looks and shopping.

Their eyes glazed over when I mentioned some of the practical considerations an editor had told me were important for beginning authors.

I began to envision someone out there with a great yearn-ing to write, who would be just as turned off by crass commercial considerations as these teachers were.

Yet in order to reach child readers and communicate with them books have to run a formidable gamut of adults—editors, librarians, buyers, parents. Books are a much more competitive business than the beginning author realizes. All authors find this out sooner or later, to their chagrin, so you will do well to learn it from the start.

I saw that I would have to follow a careful course, so as not to outrage and alienate idealistic beginning authors. My main concern must be to help you write the best book you are capable of writing. Secondary, but important, is practical help in getting your stories, thoughts, concerns, and fun to all those young readers out there. Competition? The competition begins with yourself, concentrating always to make every bit of writing better than the last.

## You'd Like to Write for Children

"I'd like to write for children." One hears it so often. Perhaps you believe that because it's for children it's easy. You know children. You may be a grandparent, a mother, a doting aunt, or a teacher. You tell them stories, sometimes making up the story as you go. You may have one story that is such a favorite they want it again and again. Surely, you think, this would make a book. If you only knew how to write it.

Actually there is no relation between telling a story to a child cuddled in your lap or snug beside you on a bed and writing a story so sharply outstanding that some editor will decide to buy it and some publisher will believe a profit can be earned by making it into a book.

The child on your lap loves your full attention, the security of your nearness, the sound and rhythm of your words. She will drink in any story you tell her.

## Practical Considerations

But producing a story you can sell brings you bang up against a long calculative process on the part of a lot of people before the story gets to the child on a lap, listening, or flat on stomach, reading. The written story must have such qualities of interest, personality, humor, and setting that some editor, a pile of manuscripts from hopeful authors on the desk, will pick yours up, read it, read it again probably with surprise and excitement because inferior submissions are the rule, then hand it on to an associate for judgment. The manuscript may be sent to an outside reviewer for a third opinion.

Practical considerations ensue. Is the story right for the age group to which the editor is responsible? Is it the right length? If this is a picture book, how costly will the artwork be? Will reviewers for newspapers and professional journals find the book worthy of notice? Will buyers for bookshops, librarians, and school supervisors who purchase books for classroom use—and who have, invariably, a tight budget—read the blurb in the publisher's catalogue, or a review, and decide to allot a bit of the precious money for its purchase?

If you want your story to be that special one picked out of the pile—and of course you do—you must accept the fact that juvenile writing is a craft to be worked at and developed to a high degree of perfection; that a writer for children must demonstrate the same skills as a writer of adult novels. Juvenile books are directed at a different audience, that's all.

This is a challenge. But tell yourself that every successful author was a beginner once. Innate talent for writing cannot be taught, but if you have the talent in some degree you can acquire the techniques necessary to truly professional writing.

Without some guidance most beginning authors do a lot of stumbling in the dark. It is the purpose of this book to set up guidelines and point the way toward a successful writing career. No one can make a finished writer of you in one small book about writing, but as you read and reread, and study your own work, you should soon see some mistakes you are making—where you have gone wrong in telling the tale or depicting the characters. Your urge to write for children should be quickened as you learn how to go about correcting those mistakes.

## Do You Know Children's Literature?

Aside from a mastery of technique there are certain qualities and abilities, background and knowledge that a serious writer for children should possess.

Juvenile literature is a branch of world literature, and the great children's books are an important and lasting part of that literature. As you work to make yourself expert, you should feel that you are not working in isolation, that you are part of an eminent clan of writers, and that your work may be destined to join the stream of children's literature that has flowed down through the centuries.

How familiar are you with the best known and best loved books for children? Your knowledge, like most people's, is probably fairly superficial. You were introduced to some stories as a child in school, by a good children's librarian or a teacher; you read books your grandmother gave you. Or you saw stories on television. A few children's classics, such as *The Wizard of Oz* by L. Frank Baum, *Charlotte's Web* by E. B. White, and *The Little Princess* by Frances Hodgson Burnett, have been quite well done on TV. But television tells the story; it seldom conveys the words that have helped to make the story live.

A fine book to take out of the library or buy for your own shelf is *A Critical History of Children's Literature* by four experts in the field of children's books. Another volume that will inspire you is *The Unreluctant Years* by Lillian H.

Smith. Published by the American Library Association, it is out of print, but a librarian can find a copy for you. Or try a used-book dealer.

## The Scope of Your World and the Child's

In my opinion, you cannot hope to become a first-rate, recognized juvenile author unless you possess some sense of world history and literary history. I do not mean that you should be writing of historical events—unless you choose to do so. But you should be on some terms of familiarity with the great past, the stirring present, the exciting stream of Oriental and Greek and Medieval and eighteenth-century and European and American history. You must, to put it bluntly, be an educated person if you are to write books for children that have substance and importance. You must write within a circle of reasonable knowledgeability.

On the other hand, as you scribble away at a story, never overlook the narrow scope of knowledge of most of today's children. Many children, an editor told me, do not know who Hitler was. Many have no notion of where China is on the map or the American Revolution or World War I, and have never heard of King Arthur.

The educators in my parlor that day said their pupils certainly do know who Hitler was and the location of China on the map. Children are very ignorant, they said, of the Bible and mythology, though they love mythology once it is presented to them.

But, one pointed out, in many schools today, especially in the old inner cities, the teacher's role has become more to maintain classroom discipline than to teach. These are the children with the narrow scope of knowledge. Never overlook them as you write. Never assume a child will understand a reference that seems common knowledge to you. But also, as you write, hope that out there some child, sitting in the background listening as the teacher reads your story, will suddenly feel a thirst to know more, the stir of an ideal that will endure, or passionately relate to the story because of some likeness to his or her life problems.

## Remembering

Juvenile authors are certainly not childish, but a good one has a quality of mind we might call childlike. You must know what is important or funny or embarrassing or heart-breaking to a child. A librarian told me that every juvenile author whom she knew had almost total recall, and perhaps this is natural equipment for a children's author. Your ability to write for children comes partly from association with children, observations of childhood, but largely it comes from remembering.

You must remember the excited anticipation as you found your seats at the circus, how you laughed out loud at the clown and gasped, hands clapped to mouth, at the perilous feats of the tightrope walkers. The bewilderment of your first day of school and the smell of apples, chalk, and fresh paint in that strange new place, the classroom. And small incidents should stand out. I remember licking my perspiring arm, probably at age four, because amazingly I had discovered my skin was salty. In memory I put my hand on my hair and feel it hot from the sun, the day we moved to New Jersey. All else of that day has faded.

Things that happen to you as an adult should bring not a blasé sigh but a genuine stir of emotion and fun and interest, so you are able to share your experience with a child reader from the child's viewpoint, not the jaded viewpoint of the average adult.

## Today's Children

Remembering, however, is not enough if you are planning to write about children of today. It has been said that children do not change—only the world around them does. But consider how this world has changed since you were a child. Those changes cannot fail to exert a powerful impact on the children of today, their attitudes and interests, and their reading.

Children now, often unsupervised, are exposed to hours of television daily—to violence, murder, thievery and trickery, pretty explicit sexual performance, and perverted notions of humor. The child who stares at the screen may have come home after school to a locked and empty house. Probably hot oatmeal for breakfast is unknown in this house; there is no gathering around the dinner table, because Mother is hurrying out to her nighttime job. Once dinner was the heart of the family group. A school principal in a poor area told me that this was one of the big problems in trying to hold families together: There was no common dinner hour, no time during the day when parents and children came together and talked.

There are, of course, homes where Mother sees the children off to school with a hug and puts a meat loaf and baking potatoes in the oven at night; where Daddy comes home to be played with and shown the fine report card. If you are writing out of an ideal personal background like this one, you must never forget those potential but hard-to-reach readers who know a different home in what may seem to you an alien and frightening world.

One way to know today's children is to volunteer in a library. Always understaffed, libraries welcome volunteers. Observe what books children take out. But many children never visit a library. One successful author I know spends one day a week in her local elementary school, where she is welcomed as author-in-residence. She helps and encourages the pupils in their writing, and in doing so she gains an insight into the variety of their homes and backgrounds and problems.

## Language

You should be well grounded in the handling of grammar and vocabulary. You should be able to express yourself with some fluency and possess the ability to choose words that will stir a reader's emotions and draw the exact reaction to your story and characters that you want. You must also be willing, as we shall discuss later in this book, to scrutinize and improve your wording, to revise; to discover in yourself a style that comes naturally and characterizes your work.

If you possess the gift for language that sets apart the world's great stories, you are fortunate indeed, but even a born writer can always improve his or her work.

The best way I know to help you recognize masterful handling of words and a distinctive style is to read the world's great literature, juvenile and adult. Good writing of any period can have a telling impact on your own work. Smile over the opening words of Jane Austen's *Pride and Prejudice:*

> It is a truth universally acknowledged that a single man in possession of a good fortune must be in want of a wife.

Read more of Jane Austen and let her quietly flowing yet brilliant and subtly humorous use of words, her skill of understatement, sink into your consciousness.

Pick up *To the Lighthouse* by Virginia Woolf, a modern if not a contemporary author:

> Now all the candles were lit up, and the faces on both sides of the table were brought nearer by the

> candle light, and composed, as they had not been in the twilight, into a party round a table, for the night was now shut off by panes of glass, which far from giving any accurate view of the outside world, rippled it so strangely that here, inside the room, seemed to be order and dry land; there, outside, a reflection in which things wavered and vanished.

Now go to Robertson Davies, a contemporary Canadian author with a genius for handling the English language. Here is the first paragraph of *A Mixture of Frailties:*

> It was appropriate that Mrs. Bridgetower's funeral fell on a Thursday, for that had always been her At Home day. As she had dominated her drawing room, so she dominated St. Nicholas Cathedral on this frosty 23rd of December. She had planned her funeral, as she had planned all her social duties and observances, with care.

You won't use language or subject matter like that when you write for children, but as you read good adult writing you will absorb the superb use of words. Turning to juvenile literature, here are some paragraphs from the ending of Beatrix Potter's *The Tailor of Gloucester:*

> He unlocked the door of the little shop in Westgate Street, and Simpkin ran in, like a cat that expects something.
>
> But there was no one there! Not even one little brown mouse!
>
> The boards were swept and clean; the little ends of thread and the little silk snippets were all tidied away, and gone from off the floor.
>
> But upon the table—oh, joy! the tailor gave a shout—there, where he had left plain cuttings of silk—there lay the most beautifulest coat and embroidered satin waistcoat that ever were worn by a

> Mayor of Gloucester. . . . Everything was finished except just one single cherry-coloured button-hole, and where that button-hole was wanting there was pinned a scrap of paper with these words—and in little teeny weeny writing—*no more twist.*

Here is a bit from a modern juvenile book, *It's like this, Cat,* by Emily Neville:

> I let Cat out of the basket and strip off my splashed shirt and chase Nick along the edge of the water. No need to worry about Cat. He chases right along with us, and every time a wave catches his feet he hisses and hightails it up the beach. Then he rolls himself in the hot dry sand and gets up and shakes. There are a few other groups of people dotted along the beach. A big mutt dog comes and sniffs Cat and gets a right and a left scratch to the nose.

And read this account, in Katherine Paterson's *Bridge to Terabithia,* of a boy's growing awareness:

> All the Burkes were smart. Not smart, maybe, about fixing things or growing things, but smart in a way Jess had never known real live people to be. Like one day while they were working, Judy came down and read out loud to them, mostly poetry and some of it in Italian, which, of course, Jess couldn't understand, but he buried his head in the rich sound of the words and let himself be wrapped warmly around in the feel of the Burkes's brilliance.

Do you recognize books for children as a branch of world literature, to be treated as seriously as any adult novel? Are you serious enough to declare a recess and take time to steep yourself in some great literature? Will you go back then and read your own work with new objectivity? Is your writing pale in comparison with what you have just read—much paler than it seemed before? Are you willing to make the great effort to bring it into the sunshine? Succeeding chapters of this book will help you do that.

## Different Editors—Different Tastes

Having said all this, I must admit that lacking a talent for language is not a fatal deterrent to writing for children. Many published books, many popular books, are not great books, reveal no genius. There are markets for all kinds of juvenile stories. Different editors have different tastes and standards, and the common view is that any book is as good as an editor thinks it is. Once there was a sharp cleavage between popular books, that bookstores sold, and books of "library quality." That distinction has pretty much disappeared. Because public libraries are for everyone, supported by taxpayers' dollars, most librarians believe they should match the books they buy with readers' interest.

The important thing is that you be willing to concentrate and study and work at improving your skill with words in a conscious effort to raise your writing above a pedestrian level. We shall go into this later in detail.

## Imagination

By imagination I do not mean simply the ability to conjure up imaginary creatures or situations. That you will do, of course. I mean the ability to imagine how your characters would think and act and talk in a situation that perhaps never happened in real life or to you personally.

If it did happen in real life and you were not there as

witness—a scene in a biography perhaps—it may be harder to picture what you imagine happened, and what people said, than it would be if you were inventing the scene.

Do you feel at home with the creatures of your imagination? Are your characters real to you? Can you project yourself into their being, know their personalities and feelings so well that you can predict and depict their actions with confidence?

## Humor

Have you a sense of humor? Do you love the ludicrous? Humor is an essential element in a book for children. It will be discussed several times in these chapters.

## Taste

By taste I mean a sense of what subject matter is fitting to write about for children of whatever age and what language is suitable. This is not just a matter of taboos or morals, although those may enter in. It is a matter of—well, taste, that's all. The same kind of judgment one exercises all the time and not just when writing for children.

The editor who decides whether or not to buy your manuscript must consider the question of good taste from the viewpoints of all the adults who select books for children. A librarian said, "I call it selection, not censorship. If I only have enough money to buy ten books, I'm going to choose authors I can depend on, not one who may spring a scene on me or some profanity in the middle of the book, that some parent is bound to complain about."

Once I bought a book that I had not read for a young

person. I came on a scene that so disgusted me I could not think of wrapping this book in pretty paper and presenting it as a birthday present. I took it back to the bookshop. The clerk looked at it, and she called out to another, "That book is back again!" They had had a number of returns.

Perhaps the scene in that book would have intrigued and titillated my young reader. He might even have thought it funny. But it never reached that reader—at least through me, an adult. I am sure there is an underground circulation of books as there is for drugs. After a few experiences like that one, a buyer for a bookshop becomes more cautious.

I once asked a high school teacher why *To Kill a Mocking Bird* by Harper Lee was included on many school reading lists.

She said, "Because it is so hard, when you're teaching the novel, to find a modern novel that every teacher can feel comfortable discussing in class."

This bit of wisdom is something to keep in mind. Envision your book for subteens being read, not at home in privacy, but aloud in a classroom.

It is also helpful to know what adults may find unappetizing, though innocent enough, but children will love. You will have to hope that those grown-ups, somewhat grudgingly, understand children. I remember a book for young children called *Angleworms on Toast.* The idea revolted me but apparently young readers thought it very funny. It comes down again to knowing the children you are writing for but keeping an eye on all those grown-ups who may stand in the way. Can you think of one special young person as you write, and gauge his or her reactions? Can you learn to attack unpleasant subjects when you think you should, yet handle them in such a way that librarian and teacher and parent will respect your treatment of those subjects, even feel that here is a book young people ought to read? Will you take the time to find out how far other juvenile authors go with profanity and questionable material? We'll say more about this later.

## Integrity

A first-rate writer for children is honest with his story, his characters, and his readers. The juvenile author who writes with tongue in cheek and no genuine feeling for the problems of children will never be a truly good writer. Children have a way of seeing what a person is really like. You may remember forming an impression of someone when you were young that proved uncannily accurate later. The person of an author comes through in what he writes. When someone says "I'd like to write kid books," I wince. That would-be author thinks that books for kids are a cinch to write and that once started can be turned out en masse, like any commodity.

In humorous writing you do often write with tongue in cheek, but here you assume that your reader is sharing the joke with you and finding it funny too.

## Do You Love to Write?

If writing is to be your career you must take joy in the work. There will be times when you would rather do anything than get down to your word processor. But when you are actually working on a story you should be so absorbed that you look at your watch and see with astonishment that you are way past lunchtime. You wake up in the morning so eager to get at your writing that you leave the bed unmade and put off your daily exercise; or the cold darkness of four A.M. may find you pounding away at some suddenly inspired revision. Friends may not see you for weeks, magazines pile up unread, and every phone call is an irritating interruption.

Someone said once that she enjoyed having traveled. Writing a book is something like that. When the book is finished, if it is a good book you enjoy having written it. But like the traveler who really did have a good time along the way, even with the frustrations of travel, you must enjoy the trip.

## Will You Be Prolific?

If you are to make a career of writing for children, you should be able to depend on a steady flow of ideas for stories. Where those ideas will come from we shall discuss, but regardless of where they come from, they must keep coming.

In my early days of writing I had more ideas for stories than I could handle—magazine stories and books. For years I wrote two picture books and one chapter-book every year. My mind was constantly alive with amusing incidents and experiences that I wanted to make and did make into stories.

After forty years or so of a busy writing life, the flow slowed. Ideas still came, but they did not strike me as fresh or worth the work of developing. Finally I stopped, or thought I had stopped, writing for publication.

I don't know about other authors, and how long they can maintain the eagerness, the compelling urge, to tell a good story. But you need not worry about that now, with years of writing before you. Just look into your thoughts, perhaps jot down all the ideas for stories or books you have stored away ready to bring out when you are ready to use them. Find out if you are well supplied. Also, you are going to find out as you read this book how to keep the ideas coming.

Often a person joins a writing class because he or she has one story—maybe that story we mentioned earlier told to a beloved child. The story may not be very good, and when the beginner reluctantly accepts that fact there is no further interest in writing.

But that manuscript that you thought at first was a good

story may contain the *seed* of some good story, which you can develop with help and advice and a lot of work. One good story is an achievement worth striving for. I shall, later, tell you the remarkable history of one small story. One good story can lead to another. If writing for children intrigues you at all, learning the craft can be an absorbing and a rewarding occupation. You may even consider it a hobby and suddenly find it is turning into much more.

## Perseverance

Finally there is something that has been said so often, seems so obvious, that I am almost embarrassed to mention it: perseverance. Perseverance is an essential not only at the beginning of your writing career but all through that career.

The difference between two beginners equally qualified to write for children is simply that one drops out early, shrugs off writing as a life work because it is not worth the effort to him. The other—and the other, I hope, is you—is fueled by inner fires. You have faith in yourself and your written words. You have bulldog determination. You will retype and send out a story again and again. This is the history of many ultimately successful books. You will take criticism and rewrite—and rewrite and rewrite—learning and improving as you go.

Hand in hand with persistence goes discipline. Can you school yourself to hours of concentration, creative thinking, and typing when you would love to be out in the sunshine? Even if you love writing, some parts of the job are drudgery.

With persistence, even with success, goes humility and the learned lesson that good writing is never easy, no matter how long you have been writing. Success, when it comes, will be the sweeter for what you have gone through to win it.

Consider these qualities necessary to a beginning author. And now begin to think too about the kind of story you would like to write. The next chapter will focus on choosing a story type.

# 2

# *Your Kind of Story*

I don't remember any conscious decision to write for two groups of children—four to eight and eight to twelve. My subteen and teenage years were a torment of shyness, and had I been making a conscious decision I might have turned into an author of books about teenagers and their problems.

But I began to have small nieces and nephews. I began to write stories about them and for them. Or were those stories for me? E. B. White, in his *Letters of E. B. White,* quotes Pamela Travers, author of *Mary Poppins,* as saying anyone who writes for children successfully is probably writing for one child—namely, the child that is himself. I had moved through young childhood in a happy glow of play and pretense. I could identify with young children. They said and did things that gave me story ideas. Most important, I found stories for little children amusing and delightful to write.

You cannot exactly lay out in advance the kind of story you want to write. To some extent you will gravitate toward a certain type of story, or events may open the way. One's life shapes one's writing. What you can do is narrow the field to the kind of story you most enjoy writing.

## Many Types of Stories

Writing for children offers a wide variety of story types. The most popular book for the average child is contemporary fiction. This field breaks down into realistic and imaginative picture books for the very young; stories of today for middle-aged children, eight to twelve; and books for subteens and teenagers, the latter known in the publishing world and libraries as young adults. From age thirteen on, readers take up adult books, but some cling to their youthful reading too. There is also fiction laid in some historic period or starring a historic figure. Fantasy, which includes science fiction, is popular at all levels. Nonfiction in its many forms will be discussed in a separate chapter.

If you are writing a little for this age and a little for that, or different kinds of stories, as soon as you comfortably can you should settle into one or two story forms that you enjoy working in, and make yourself expert. Successful authors, or most of them, find a niche and stay in it.

Until you find your own métier, you will achieve no identity as an author. The experience you gain in one background, the facility and skill you achieve, are wasted if you move to a different arena. The editors who read your manuscripts put you down as a jack of all trades and master of none.

## Favorite Authors

Don't you remember, when you were a child, how eagerly you searched the library shelves for another book by a favorite author? You settled down with a cozy thrill of anticipation. I adored the *Little Colonel* books by Annie Fellowes Johnston, and I remember a birthday when one present was a *Little Colonel* book. That day I was taken for a day trip on a Hudson River liner as a special birthday treat, but I sat on deck, eyes glued to the book, for the entire journey up and down the river.

A child's favorite author is the one whose books he or she has come to love and eagerly look forward to, and if that author switches to an entirely different sort of story the child reader may put the library book back on the shelf in disappointment, turn away, and look for another favorite author.

This is one reason for the popularity of the "series" books. The children who go into a library and take out one after another read them because they know exactly what to expect. The pattern is familiar and comfortable. These books may be production-line products, and lacking in literary worth, but they teach the lesson that staying with one type of story can be an element of success; financial success, that is. It is possible to some extent to be a literary success without being a financial success, but it is nice to be both. That is what we are aiming at in this book.

There is a difference between writing "series" books and simply doing several books about the same character. Series books carry the implication of a stereotyped hero or heroine doing stereotyped things—solving a mystery, perhaps.

A character who is consistent and real in his or her person and has a fresh, original adventure in every book is quite a different matter. There are eight books about my ghost, Gus, each a distinctively different ghost experience. The latest, *Gus Loved His Happy Home,* appeared in 1989, and news of a new Gus book brought cheers from a group of first-graders who knew the other Gus books. Fondness for the older books will boost a new one, and vice versa.

## Draw from Your Own Background

It seems hard for beginning writers to draw on material from their own backgrounds. This may be due to blindness to the seemingly commonplace. The familiar is too close.

In a class I taught in juvenile writing there was a girl whose family owned a campground where two hundred families came every summer. Think of the stories, the human situations, among all those people. The setting she knew by heart. She had enough material in that campground to spend her life writing about. She couldn't see it; she insisted on writing about baby raccoons. Baby raccoons would be a delightful subject for some writer, but here it seemed a sad waste of marvelous story material.

Another girl in the class knew a lot about horses, but she wasn't writing about horses. A musician joined the class, eager to write fantasy. Later I learned that he had a musician son with whom some problems had arisen. There was material here for a book, but he never considered writing it or even thought about it as book material.

Whether your own background seems drab, or colorful and meaningful when you use it in a book depends on what you see in it and what you can reveal to the reader.

When I say your background I mean everything that makes up a milieu. Suppose you have a yen to write a juvenile book laid on year-round Cape Cod. You must know what kind of people live there; that the world of working Cape Codders is different from the world of summer folk and all the retired wash-ashores. You must know what sort of work the fathers and mothers of your child characters do. You must know that in winter the grown-ups sing in choruses, run church suppers, serve, perhaps, on a school or recreation committee. You must be familiar with how they act at town meeting, what they say at the supper table about their selectmen and summer people. You must know what time they eat, and the food dished out. Even though you are writing for children and about children, you must know the background in which your book characters live, so you can move comfortably inside your story.

You must know that the young folks play hockey, go camping with the Boy Scouts, find jobs in summer, padlock their bicycles, and ride on the school bus. One author who drew on her own background was Johanna Spyri. Mrs. Spyri grew up in an Alpine village in Switzerland, and she used that setting and episodes of her childhood in the enduring classic *Heidi.*

An exotic background is the last thing a book for children needs. The most popular of the realistic children's books are laid in an ordinary home, whether or not the kind of home many of us grew up in. If you have lived in Laos and are dying to write a book with that background, you should try, because children need to learn about distant places. But write about a place you know and can bring to life for your readers, not one you have to read up on or imagine.

One particular kind of story may come naturally to you right from the start. You are probably trying to write in that genre right now. You love funny little tales of imaginary animals, picture-book subjects. Real animal adventures may intrigue you. Perhaps you find the problems of today's teen-agers compelling. Or memories of your own middle-aged childhood may be so vivid that you yearn to put them into a story. Whatever your choice of age group and story type, you must, as I said earlier, enjoy the writing. If you can convey your own pleasure and excitement in what you are writing about, readers will enjoy it too.

Perhaps you will decide to go to the library and find the shelves of juvenile books. Ask the librarian to pull out some popular books in the field that appeals to you. Scan a few books for other ages, too, to find out what has been written, what is being written, and what children like to read. This will give you a perspective you will never acquire just sitting at your desk in a kind of vacuum, writing. If you go at a quiet hour you will find the librarian glad to talk with you about books and what a librarian looks for when buying books.

If you long to write a biography or a fictional novel about some figure in history, look in *Books in Print* to see whether someone else has got there before you. An earlier book would not necessarily rule out your own, but you would need to read the other one and decide whether you could write a better book or one with a fresh interpretation of the character.

## Are There Any Norms?

Contemporary juvenile fiction takes many forms. You will discover that current books do not follow any norm, so you have a wide latitude as you begin to consider settling into your own kind of book.

But there is a norm among popular children's books of other years that are just as loved today as they ever were. Hundreds of books written years ago have a new life now in hard cover or paperback. Authorities in the field of children's literature will tell you that one reason for the surge of revival is that so few good books are being written. If you can write a really good book there's a market out there.

I am going to try and teach you the general pattern of the classic children's story. As one must learn some basics in music, so must you in writing. The guidelines are intended to help you write a good story, not to hedge you in. They are not—God forbid—a formula. They are not rules. They will be valuable if you are a serious beginner, but once you become proficient they should slip into your subconscious and you will not be aware of following guidelines any more than you are aware, when you ice-skate, of instructions you had when you were learning.

All right, you are beginning to think about the kind of stories you will most enjoy writing. You need ideas for those stories. Let's consider where the ideas will come from and how an idea grows into a book.

# 3

# Ideas and How They Grow

Some authors, I hear, sit at their word processors and the juices start to flow. In my experience an idea usually came when I was busy about other things and thinking least about writing. Activity other than writing that involves mental effort—perhaps a tough job in a volunteer organization—seems to make the mind extraordinarily active and fertile.

As you become a published author you will suffer when you do not have an idea for a story. You are positive you will never have another. You tell people you have no ideas, and they retort, "You said that last year," and point to the book you have just had published.

Eventually you will learn that those people are right. You will also learn that such suffering is an occupational disease and that, when least expected, an article in the paper or a chance remark will give you something to work with. But if you are a born writer the creative urge never gives you a moment's peace except in intervals when you settle down with a juicy idea or when you have just finished or sold a story.

## Ideas from Every Day

Everything is grist for an author's mill, and any simple activity may produce an idea. I was painting the kitchen and observed that fresh walls made the rest of the room dingy when the idea of one improvement leading to another took form in a story, *The Magic Geranium.* I looked at new houses with the thought of moving out of an old one, and home began to look pretty good; I wrote *Mrs. Krause Finds a House.* I hunted for a cricket that kept throwing its voice around the kitchen, and dusted corners as I went. Amused, I wrote *The Cricket That Cleaned House.*

Taking my mother to visit Williamsburg, a small boy in a restaurant en route, whom I heard but never saw, produced *Andy and Mr. Cunningham.* I was giving a talk at a PTA meeting when a mother told me about her little boy, Lennie, who said he was a dog and wanted his lunch on the floor. That gave me *Lunch for Lennie.*

One of my most popular picture books was *The Blueberry Pie Elf.* I had inadvertently left a blueberry pie on a kitchen counter overnight, and in the morning there were tiny blue footprints around it. A mouse. No! I decided. An elf! An elf who liked blueberry pie so much he hoped I would bake another. But how could he tell me? Recently I have had several passionate pleas, one a phone call from California, for a copy of *The Blueberry Pie Elf.* The man from California had read it to his children, now he wanted it for his grandchildren. A young woman wrote that the book had been part of her life. As a child she had again and again cleaned the house when her mother was out so Mother would say, "We must have an elf around here!" Now she wanted the book for the children she was teaching.

One night, playing bridge, a friend remarked, "I forgot to feed the outside cats." Who were the outside cats, I asked. "Oh, they stay around but I never let them in." A story, I thought. An outside cat that wants to be an inside cat. I wrote *The Outside Cat.*

The *Cat That Joined the Club* came from kindly cousins who left a box, with a lining of old Persian carpet, in their breezeway for a cat that came and went.

I visited a niece who was working with VISTA in South Carolina. "Down that road," she said, "there's a mysterious light." In a later chapter I'll tell you about the long, questing trail that led to *Ginnie and the Mystery Light.*

Another popular book, *Ginnie and the Mystery House,* grew out of a real visit, like the one in the book, from a fearful old lady.

And I remember the night when it suddenly occurred to me I had a picture book in a game I played with two small visiting nieces. They stayed right behind me, giggling, while I exclaimed, "Where *are* those girls?" and looked down the sink and under the rug. I was so excited I couldn't sleep and I wrote *Where's Andy?* A new idea is a thrilling experience for a juvenile author.

This list could go on and on. Some ideas come to you unbidden. Others, as a friend put it, you must step out to get. Years ago, when I had had just one book published, I decided to take a course in juvenile writing. It would have been easier on those winter nights to go home after a day's work instead of trekking way downtown to a class. But one assignment was to write a description of two very different children. I chose myself and my best friend in fourth grade. Another pupil in the class remarked, "You almost have a book there." I saw that I had, and I expanded the description into *Ginnie and Geneva.* My teacher became my editor and my entire career grew out of that course in juvenile writing. Quite aside from all I learned is the fact that I made the effort to take the course.

## Other Authors' Ideas

Feeling foolish, because "Where do you get your ideas?" is a stock question, I queried some fellow writers.

Nancy Dingman Watson has written many books for children and has eight children of her own. Yes, she said, some of her books have been sparked by her children. But most have come from her own childhood. She cited two poems from her slim volume *Blueberry Lavender. My Cat* is an exact account of a childhood experience, and *My Own Room* is a true memory.

For one book, *New Under the Stars,* Nancy Watson drew on a trip she had made with her children, but for the purpose of the story she exchanged her own family for a sharecropper's family. As a teenager she had worked with sharecroppers and she had that experience to draw on.

One of her books came straight from her youngest child. Tommy announced that Muncus Agruncus, a bad little mouse, had thrown his father downstairs. Tommy saw him do it. His mother wrote *Muncus Agruncus, A Bad Little Mouse.* In the book Muncus does not throw his father downstairs, but he does lots of other bad things. As can often be the case, the idea of a bad little mouse was all the author took. She went on with her own devising.

Nancy Watson's daughter, Clyde Watson, is also an author, and she told me how her book *Tom Fox and the Apple Pie* started.

"I was teaching six-year-olds in an ungraded school, and trying to teach them a little elementary math. One day they were restless; they didn't want to do fractions, they wanted a story. I made up a story about Tom Fox, who bought a pie and planned to share it with some relatives. The number of relatives kept growing smaller and smaller, and Tom ended up eating the whole pie." By that time Clyde had conveyed a little understanding of fractions. "Most of my books," she says, "come from things that happen."

In *Letters of E. B. White* that author tells how *Charlotte's Web* came to be: "The idea of writing *Charlotte's Web* came to me one day when I was on my way down through the orchard carrying a pail of slops to my pig. I had made up my mind to write a children's book about animals, and I needed a way to save a pig's life, and I had been watching a large spider in the backhouse, and what with one thing and another, the idea came to me."

As for Charlotte, the spider, he says, "I didn't like spiders at first, but then I began watching one of them and soon saw what a wonderful creature she was and what a skillful weaver. I named her Charlotte, and now I like spiders along with everything else in nature."

I asked Jean Fritz, author of many juvenile biographies, about her ideas and she said, "It seems to me that ideas are generated by what kind of person the writer is. A newspaper piece that would strike one person as a potential story would hold no interest for another. Beginning writers, it seems to me, make the mistake of looking outside themselves, of trying to model their stories on clichés of old stories or on television material. A writer has, first of all, to know himself (or herself), then to be in touch with his own childhood."

## Search Your Life

If ideas for books simply do not come to you from daily doings, you might deliberately search your life. Analyze several experiences of your childhood. Why were they important? How did they turn out? Could you make them work out differently in a story? What really happened may not be enough; you will need to expand and invent. And don't just remember what happened; remember how you felt.

It is possible to adapt an adult experience for use in a juvenile book. I took part in a local political campaign and learned a lot about small-city politics and how a campaign is run. I enjoyed the excitement and suspense so much that I yearned to write about it, but how was I going to involve children in politics? Then I saw boys playing ball in the street, perilously close to my windows. Why not have some boys campaign for a candidate who would give them a ball field? *David's Campaign Buttons* turned out well, and my experience lent realism.

Once I was a stringer for *The New York Times,* pasting up

my little local stories every month and receiving a small check. I utilized this experience when I wrote *Cathy Leonard Calling*.

I read a book about luck that made a good point. Luck, it conjectured, is often associated with people one encounters. Something good happens, a bit of so-called luck, through someone you meet.

The more people you meet, then, the more likely you are to be lucky with ideas. An author needs an inflow of ideas, and the person who comes in contact with many people and constantly has new experiences probably has more ideas coming in than the recluse.

It is important for authors to observe people. Notice how they act, hear what they say and how they say it, and perceive whether the way a person acts has significance larger than that one person. Is this a prototype of a modern grandmother? An ever-in-action little boy?

## No Idea Comes Complete

An idea may be nothing more than a character, remark, tone of voice, a gesture that haunts you. To some such fragment you add a piece from an incident on the street, a newspaper piece, or a friend's chance remark. Some of these you may jot down, others your memory stores away. The mind is a wonderful catalyst, and somehow it brings all the elements together at the appointed time.

## Is It a Good Idea?

How do you know whether it's a good idea? Live with it for a while. Think about it as you take a walk or lie in bed at dawn. Can you see a plot there that would interest children? Is it a story? People are always saying, "I have an idea for you," but that is usually a fragment that fails to suggest a good story.

Occasionally people do offer useful hints. A friend said, "My husband has been telling the boys a story about a dragon that can pop corn." I have no idea what those stories for the boys were, but after a tussle with the story line I wrote *The Popcorn Dragon.* A librarian told me she had a child reader who was terrified of wolves. Would I please write about a good wolf. I did.

Check your idea against certain child emotions a story should appeal to: love of fun, of adventure and mystery, loyalty, caring, the desire to be brave and to be kind, to overcome problems and rise to greater heights. To be a hero.

A teacher told me she had observed in her young pupils, many of whom came from broken homes, a fear of abandonment. She wondered if this could explain the long continued success of my little book *The Puppy Who Wanted a Boy*.

Children enjoy reading about others like themselves, but they also respond strongly to a book about children with happier family relationships and in more affluent circumstances. Such stories feed their dreams and aspirations.

I have had hundreds of letters from little girls who adore *Ginnie and Geneva* for its feeling of warmth and security. One child who had some serious family griefs told me, "I've read it eighteen times!" And a friend said that her grown-up daughter had marital problems, "and when she is really depressed she reads one of your books."

Little children love imaginative stories about animals. An idea must possess freshness. Avoid anything that has been done over and over again—the lost dog, the dream. The forever popular little-old-woman story should have a child-like little old character, so that small readers will feel protective. To be saleable it would also need a strikingly original and entertaining plot.

A librarian told me that most subteen books are directed

at girls; she wished someone would write a good book for boys of that age. Girls read books about boys and, contrary to what some teachers tell me, boys do read girls' books. The girls who have loved Ginnie owe a debt to one boy. Before *Ginnie and Geneva* became a book it ran as a serial in a juvenile magazine. When the last installment had been published and the magazine began a new serial, a boy wrote to the publisher. Please, he begged, "go back to *Ginnie and Geneva.* It was a much better story than the one you're running now." They sent the letter on to me, and for the first time it occurred to me that I might write another book about Ginnie. Thanks to "Your friend, Harvey," seven books about Ginnie appeared.

Unless you are a technician or scientist, don't try a technical or scientific subject right away. Readers like science fiction, but wait until your technique has been perfected. An editor might question your expertise in the field and some smart young reader might know more than you do.

The historical novel? We shall go into historical fiction and its special requirements in a later chapter.

## Is There Humor in Your Idea?

Children love to laugh, and the parts of a book they say they like best when they write fan letters are the funny parts. We'll say more about humor later. Humor is essential in books for the very young, and stories for any age, no matter how serious, are better for some leaven of laughter. Parents and teachers who read to children like to laugh too. They won't tire of reading your book if it's funny.

## A Universal Quality

A good children's book, except for mystery or adventure, has a truth, a universal quality, a theme, call it what you will, underlying the plot. If your story is about a lonely child, such as Ginnie, your reader will tell you that in the book Ginnie went to school for the first time and hated Geneva, who made fun of her, but then she and Geneva became friends and she liked school. If someone asks you, the author, what the book is about, you may say it is the story of a child wanting to be part of society. Both of you would be right.

But a theme is useless without a good story for a vehicle. No editor will take a book of fiction unless it tells a good story. You, the author, should not be aware of any theme. An idea appeals to you. You write the story and discover if you look hard enough that it has something to say beyond the story, and that is why the idea appealed to you and why it is a good story. Perhaps *theme* is too pompous a word. I mean an experience that children and parents who read aloud will recognize.

A family I knew moved into a house where a little girl had a room of her own for the first time. I wondered what would happen if she had to give up the precious room. I wrote *A Room for Cathy*. The story was serialized in a magazine and the magazine received more fan mail than it had ever received about a story. Every little girl longs for a room of her own. I had been thinking in terms of a good story, but the universal appeal was what made the book so successful.

## Relevance Has Weight

Many books loved by children for years have no particular relevance to life today, but relevance has weight when you evaluate an idea for a new book. Add the quality of timeliness to a good story and lifelike characters, and so much the better. You may be familiar with the problem of drug use among teenagers, the one-parent family, or the potentials of a computer. Maybe you know that a certain little girl would rather have false fingernails than a doll for Christmas; that is an important insight. Editors are receptive to a manuscript that relates to today, and if the story is powerful enough I suspect an editor might overlook some deficiencies in the writing.

## Getting into the Mood

I have talked about the importance of reading in expanding your knowledge of the world and of children's literature. Now I want to talk about your reading from a different aspect. Reading great books can help to stir creativity, quicken your eagerness to express your ideas in words of your own, or so it seems to me. If you find an author who especially stirs you, read everything that author has written. Dorothy Canfield, in her novels and short stories, wrote the sort of thing I would like to write if I were writing for adults, and it may have been her juvenile, *Understood Betsy,* that created the first stirring of desire in me to write *Ginnie and Geneva.*

The wonderful simplicity of Willa Cather has the same effect. She does not tell me what to write, but she creates a mental or spiritual climate in which my ideas are likely to prick through the ground. Reading English and Irish folk tales, I feel the soil of my mind turned over by the creative impulse.

I believe that for any good imaginative writing this condition of excitement, of heightened perceptiveness and sensitivity, is necessary. Some days the brain is dull and sterile. On those days it would be a waste of time to try and write. Other days the mind is full of exciting possibilities. This mood does not always produce a story; it may fade before you can seize any of the will-o'-the-wisps floating beyond your grasp.

But one thing seems certain to me. You must create this mood or you will not produce a story. Reading the best fiction that has been written—not juvenile fiction necessarily—will help.

## You Need Time

When you find yourself in the idea stage of writing a book, you need time. Time to grasp the idea that has come to you, that you have become convinced is a good, usable idea; to nourish it in your mind until it has grown into much more than an idea.

It is said that people utilize about fifty percent of their mental capacity. It takes a hundred percent, I am convinced, to be an author. The sternest self-discipline is required. You must sit down quietly, control wandering thoughts. It is not easy. Your mind goes off on every possible tangent and refuses to focus on the problem at hand. Eyes stray, you doodle.

But gradually, as you make yourself sit in absolute quiet and freedom from distraction, the disturbing elements begin to drop away. At last you begin to think clearly and you experiment with your story idea. Pen or pencil in hand helps. You may scribble an outline, scratch it out, scribble another and another.

Only when you feel pretty clear about where you want to go with your story idea do you start writing a synopsis of a book.

It happens sometimes that you hit a block and you put your idea aside, convinced there is something there but unable to see what you should do with it. This happened to me with *Mr. Turtle's Magic Glasses.* The solution may appear after your subconscious thought processes have helped or other events or ideas have come along to relate to it. Or after you have produced easier stories. People ask, "How long does it take to write a book?" Several weeks or months. Sometimes years. Meanwhile you may turn out several other stories.

Let us assume you do have a good idea for a book. That idea can only be developed through some fictional people or animals, whom you must invent. So we come to one of the most important elements of your book, the characters.

# 4

# The People in Your Book

In a doctor's waiting room I picked up a copy of *Time,* struck by the words on the cover. "Through the Eyes of Children," I read. "Growing up in America Today."

Juvenile authors try to see life through the eyes of children. As I read about the five young people whose lives were discussed in *Time,* I saw that any one of them would make a book.

Many of the juveniles being written today are about children in families quite different from the typical family of a generation ago. On the floor beside my typewriter towers a pile of books. In Cynthia Voigt's *A Solitary Blue* the boy lives with his father; his mother has walked out. Phoebe in *The Divorce Express* by Paula Danziger commutes weekends between father and mother. In Barbara Corcoran's *Me and You and a Dog Named Blue,* Maggie's mother is dead.

In *Cracker Jackson* by Betsy Byars the parents are divorced, and Cracker lives with his mother but remains on good telephone terms with his father. Jerry in *The Chocolate War* by Robert Cormier lives with his father after his mother's death.

Even in a lighthearted younger book, *The Amazing Memory of Harvey Bean* by Mollie Cone, Harvey's parents are separated. Harvey isn't sure what happiness is, but separation of parents seems to be a fairly normal thing that he can live with.

Only in *Bridge to Terabithia* is there a solid two-parent family, there are two of them, in fact.

## Your Choice of Characters

At the moment we are looking at these situations not from the viewpoint of a story but with an eye to the characters you may choose to work with when you write a juvenile book. It is important to recognize that social scene and attitudes have changed dramatically. Not all mothers and fathers are married; some have been married more than once. One parent or the other is missing in many families.

If a mother-father family remains intact, Mother may be a teacher, a cashier in a supermarket, or a nurse who works at night and is sleeping when the children come home from school. There are fathers who have assumed the role of homemaker. A family may be a mixture of offspring from former marriages or include adopted children of varying national backgrounds.

Boys still do boy things and girls do girl things, but Maggie in *Me and You and a Dog Named Blue* has made the ball team at school. Jesse, age ten, in *Bridge to Terabithia,* loves to draw pictures, adores a youthful teacher who loves art too, and enters spontaneously into the world of magic and make-believe with his friend Leslie.

## What About the Happy Home?

The girls in my own books live in happy homes. I assumed that the tranquil, affectionate household I grew up in was typical. As an adult, I learned from reminiscences of peers that it was not; that in some of the seemingly happy homes of my friends ghosts lurked in the shadows. But there are happy homes, and there is nothing unrealistic about creating characters who live in such homes.

## The Character Makes the Story

A book for children of any age is usually about children, especially about one child character, and the story will be the story it is because of the nature of the child you have chosen as your chief character.

You the author feel strongly about this character, real or imaginary, or you would not be writing the book. Are you writing about a girl? Do you love this child? Do you feel she needs help in some way? Maybe she amuses or exasperates you, or both. Your problem is to get her down on paper so your readers see her just as you do and feel the same as you feel about her. They must come to care strongly about what happens to her.

## Know Your Child Character

Before you start writing about this girl you yourself must be absolutely clear about her. No fuzzy impressions. You must know her better than you know your sister because you must know what goes on in her head and in her heart. You also need to know how old she is, how tall, what color eyes, how her hair grows, what sort of parents and home she has. All about her temperament, likes and dislikes, sense of humor, talents, ambitions, and IQ.

You think about all this until it sinks into your subconscious. You will never pass all this background information on to your readers in so many words, but you will know your girl so well that you will never make her act in an unnatural way or put words in her mouth she would not use.

If your character is based on a real child you are probably very familiar with that boy or girl. It is seldom, however, that you can make a book character exactly like the real-life person. Circumstances in your book will no doubt be different from the life circumstances in which you know the child, so you will keep the real child in your head but adapt for the purpose of your story.

From the start you must clearly delineate that child and the other important characters. In *Bridge to Terabithia* you know Jesse from the first page. He gets up at dawn to run and has run so much that his feet are as tough as his old sneakers. As his younger sister May Belle wakes up to ask where he is going he pats her hair and pulls the sheet up to her chin. He whispers that he is just going to run the cow field, and she smiles and snuggles down. You like this boy.

Before chapter one is finished you have a good picture of Momma, a tired, hard-working, good countrywoman who wants her children to be decent. She orders Jesse to put his shirt on for breakfast. When she tells the girls, "You ain't got no money for school shopping," you know the status of the family, and you learn more about Momma as, after all, she counts out five wrinkled bills.

You can see Brenda, an older sister, as "holding her nose, her pinky delicately crooked," she complains that Jesse stinks. It is clear May Belle adores her brother, not only from the waking-up incident but because she trots off to fetch his T-shirt.

As I read this book I waited anxiously for Daddy to come home, I so wanted him to be a good father. I was not disappointed. May Belle screams "Daddy!" with delight as he drives in in his pickup truck, and her father unlatches the door for her to climb in and be hugged.

Now you know this family, this set of characters. You know them because the author has, consciously or unconsciously, employed several techniques.

## Your Principal Character

One technical point is how to show early in the story who your principal character is. I had a discussion about this with some seventh-graders. I told them a reader should be able to identify the main character on the first page. One of them asked, "If three people are mentioned how do you know which it is?" Probably the first one who appears. The main character should be involved in some action or dialogue or thinking right at the start.

## *Technique of the Single Viewpoint*

There is one all-important way to distinguish the main character. It is known as the technique of the single viewpoint. As author, your job is not to act as a commentator reporting a ball game; your job is to take the reader inside the main character so that he becomes the ballplayer and plays the game. Reader identification, this is called. The single viewpoint, that of your lead character, and reader identification are especially important in juvenile books because children, perhaps unconsciously, want to be that boy or girl in the story.

Your leading character is the only one author and reader get inside of. Just as in real life one must judge people by what they look like, what they say, and how they act, so it should be with the other characters in your book.

In *A Solitary Blue* the reader becomes intimately involved with Jeff's thoughts and emotions, but all one knows about Jeff's father, Professor Greene, is from what he says and does. The reader's feeling about this man changes as he begins to act differently toward his son and as Jeff gradually grows to see him in a new light. But you never once penetrate the inner recesses of the Professor's thought processes.

In *Me and You and a Dog Named Blue* you know that Maggie's father is displeased with her poor report card because he says, "Well, that was a stinker, wasn't it?" You know how he feels about her making the ball team when he throws the card on the table and says, "I'm sorry you ever made that lousy team." And when Aunt Myrt drives up and he hides Maggie's report card and says, "Hang up the dishtowel, quick. Put away the dishes in the drainer. If the place is a mess I'll hear about it from hell to breakfast," you know something about his relationship with his sister and something about Aunt Myrt.

*The Call of the Wild* provides a study in the technique of the single viewpoint. Here the viewpoint is that of the dog hero. Human characters come and go; they are clear-cut people shown by their appearance, their words and actions. The dog's viewpoint guides the story, keeping it on a straight track, and the remarkable detailing of the changes in an animal's viewpoint and approach to life and survival produces a powerful and gripping story.

Once understood, this technique is not at all difficult to use, yet it escapes many beginning authors. Just watch to be sure you never write from any viewpoint except your main actor's.

Single viewpoint can be handled in either first person or third person. This is a matter of choice on your part. Experiment with "I," then with "he" or "she" and find out which comes more easily. If the story is based on an intimate personal experience, such as Yoko Kawashima Watkins's *So Far From the Bamboo Grove* and Jean Fritz's *Homesick,* first person will come naturally. If you write in the first person you will be less likely to stray into another character's thoughts. But third person is the medium of the natural storyteller.

## *Exceptions to the Rule*

There is no rule in editorial offices that says, "Can't buy any book that doesn't have a single viewpoint." I think of two books that break the rule with great effectiveness. *The*

*Pinballs* by Betsy Byars presents three viewpoints. Carlie's is preeminent because she is the strongest character and prime mover of the action. The two boys are often shown through action and speech but their thoughts do come through and no difficult shift of viewpoint on the reader's part seems called for. This is because your sympathy runs so deep with all three.

And in *The Chocolate War* Robert Cormier injects the emotional reactions of a cross-section of the boys trapped into mad Brother Leon's campaign to sell chocolates. Probably in no other way could the scope of the chocolate war have been sketched so graphically.

Archie's evil angle on the enterprise is shown again and again. There is the Goober, fifteen years old and a beautiful runner, but terrified to tears by the destructive prank he is bullied into. John Sulkey, anxious to get on an honor roll if only for selling chocolates; Tubs Casper, mad to earn money; Caroni, whom Brother Leon is blackmailing. Vignettes depict the role of each in the chocolate war. Yet periodically the reader is returned to Jerry, whose misery and determination run like a thread through the narrative.

Brother Leon, kingpin of the whole affair, is shown in all his demonic madness from outside, from the view of others. This treatment, separate from that of the boys, gives the book a unity it might not possess had Brother Leon been thrown in with his victims.

These are rare exceptions. But this you may be sure of: An editor knows a good story when it shows up. In stressing the single viewpoint I am sharing perhaps the most important secret that goes into the writing of a well-plotted, well-told tale that will grip the reader's interest.

## The Five Senses

If the young reader is to identify closely with your character you must make that reader not only think but feel, smell, taste, hear, and see along with the child in the story. Heat, cold, muscle strains, pain reach out to draw your reader inside the character and the story.

## Feeling

As Jesse in *Bridge to Terabithia* trots across the yard in early morning, the reader can see his breath coming out in little puffs, and later feels and hears the flies around his sweating face. The reader feels the heat in the kitchen where his mother is canning beans and the icy splash of mud on Jesse's and Leslie's legs as they run to their secret spot. These are recognizable sensations.

The opening words of *The Chocolate War* describe what happens to Jerry in a ball game:

> As he turned to take the ball, a dam burst against the side of his head and a hand grenade shattered his stomach. Engulfed by nausea, he pitched toward the grass. His mouth encountered gravel, and he spat frantically, afraid that some of his teeth had been knocked out. Rising to his feet, he saw the field through drifting gauze but held on until everything settled into place. Like a lens focussing, making the world sharp again, with edges.

These are vivid impressions that the reader shares even though he has not lived through that experience himself.

## Smell and Taste

Use smell and taste to the hilt. Smell is the most nostalgic of the senses, instantly invoking a memory. A boy in a book sniffs the cold spicy scent of balsam and Christmas wells up in the reader. Ginnie and friends make fudge, chocolatey fragrance filling the air; the reader is smelling that fudge. Have your heroine come home to chicken roasting or potatoes baking; your reader is in the kitchen, hungry for dinner.

Where there is food there is taste. Young people love to eat, they're always eating. The child reading your book will be one with the heroine who is crunching buttered popcorn, sipping hot cocoa after an evening of play in new snow, or biting into a juicy apple as she starts her homework.

## *Hearing*

The sense of hearing is especially useful when you want a feeling of eeriness. In my *Look Alive, Libby* Aunt Paula has ended the agony of a trapped mouse in the attic in a pail of water. At a later date, in the house with only a tired, snoring old lady, Libby hears a familiar sound overhead:

> . . . When the thumping began to penetrate her consciousness some time in the black hours it took her a long while to rouse enough to know she was hearing it. Gradually her senses sharpened. *Thump. Thump.* . . In a rush of awareness Libby was wide awake. The mouse in the trap . . . It couldn't be! Not with Aunt Paula away! *Thump.* If she pulled the covers over her head perhaps the noise would stop . . . *Thump. Thump.*

In *Libby's Uninvited Guest* she has a similar experience:

> Then suddenly she was awake. There had been a sound over her head. Mice again, of course . . . As long as they stayed in the attic they didn't worry Libby. Sleep, so close, had retreated. Her drowsy senses were alert, listening for the mice. And the sound came again. Disquiet stirred in Libby. Little

> light mouse feet scampered, but the sounds she was hearing were solid . . . She was taut with listening as the noise came again. This time it sounded like a human foot set cautiously on the old floorboards over her head.

## *Sight*

The visual sense you will employ most often. In *A Solitary Blue* Jeff sits on the end of the dock and looks around:

> Behind him on the low rise of land that passed as a hill in this flat country, the house sat, its windows bright. Before him, the creek ran slowly, the long field of marshes swayed like waves under a breeze not strong enough to do more than rustle the leaves on the trees. A great blue paced its territory down to the west, toward the bay, where little waves rippled.

All this is seen through Jeff's eyes.

*Heidi* contains lovely passages describing the Alpine meadows, always as Heidi sees them:

> Heidi jumped here and there and shouted for joy; for there were whole troops of delicate primroses together, and yonder it was blue with gentians, and everywhere in the sunshine smiled and nodded the tender-leaved rockroses.

Heidi breathes the air filled with fragrance of flowers, sees the wind toss the blossoms, and feels a deep stillness. Color, scent, the tactile reaction to fresh air and the stirring of wind mingle to create a many-dimensioned feeling of the Alpine meadows. The reader's reaction will blend with Heidi's ecstasy.

# Exposition

You may encounter an impulse to write in the expository form, tell the story yourself instead of letting your characters tell it through their own words or actions. Be on guard about this. Once I wanted to describe in my own words a small boy in my book. My editor wouldn't let me. "You are writing from that little boy's viewpoint," she said, "and he never sees himself. Unless he looks in the mirror, and little boys are too busy to look in the mirror." Before I had finished writing chapter one I knew what David looked like. So did the readers, although their images were no doubt different from mine. It was a useful lesson.

If you the author feel you must resort to describing a character, often a clue will be enough—a little girl chewing absentmindedly on the end of a pigtail, a boy walking with a crutch. Let the picture build up in the reader's imagination as it did in the old radio programs. Break up your expository description, slip it in, combine it with action and dialogue.

In the following simple example from *Ginnie and Her Juniors* there is one expository sentence, the first. I did not need to say Susan was a shy little girl; the way Susan acts tells the reader.

> Mrs. Fraser's small daughter Susan was three. She came to the door behind her mother, peering round her skirt with big brown eyes. Ginnie looked down at the chubby and adorable little figure, the red-gold hair and pink cheeks, and fell in love at first sight. Susan, however, retired to the other side of the room and rejected advances.

## Action

This brings us to action, which is illustrated in the example just given. Action is the best way of all to show what a character is like because it is part of the fabric of your narrative and carries the story on. What a character does tells a lot about him or her.

I quoted the opening of *The Chocolate War*. That first paragraph does more than unite the reader with Jerry. This boy, only fourteen, is down and almost out as the result of rough treatment in the ball game. Yet he staggers to his feet, in pain, breathless, barely conscious. He wants to sink down again and he does. But when he hears the coach call his name, wondering how he is going to get up with both legs, he thinks, smashed, and his skull battered in, he finds himself on his feet.

All of that is important because the doggedness of this boy is going to make his resistance to the evil school organization believable later on.

On a lighter note, let me turn again to one of my own books, *A Room for Cathy:*

> Jeffy appeared, crawling on the floor and pushing a truck. "Er, er, er, er, er," Jeffy chugged, ignoring his sister and her friend, his face pink as he bent over the truck.

The action in its context not only pictures this little boy; his deliberate intrusion points up the lack of privacy that his sister Cathy finds painful in the small apartment. This is important to the story.

As for Jeff's two sisters, a little action tells something about each:

> Chris left the room without more ado, also without combing her hair. Cathy shook her head over

> her departing sister as she got out clean underclothes and robed herself in suitable fashion for this great occasion. She combed her hair, parting it carefully and pinning it trimly into place with a red barrette. Then, surrounded by a strong aura of Summer Garden toilet water, she emerged into the midst of the movers.

The following action presents Jeff and Cathy and their relation to one another:

> She could see her door opening softly as the light from the hall shone in. Someone stood there, motionless. Then, as Cathy stirred, a small, sturdy figure pattered across the floor toward her. "I had a bad dream. I want to get in your bed," Jeff said. "All right, Jeffy, come on." Cathy moved over and he scrambled quickly under the covers to snuggle against her. She covered him and he moved confidently closer, his solid little back warm against her . . . Cathy put her arm around her little brother.

When you master the handling of action that not only characterizes someone in the book but also moves the story ahead, you will have come a long way toward becoming a successful storyteller.

## Dialogue

An essential of good characterization is dialogue. Right at the start a bit of dialogue can show what kind of person your chief character is. Maggie in *Me and You and a Dog Named Blue* faces up to her father about her poor report card, and you know by page two what a feisty youngster she is. She describes her teacher as an "ass-hole" and her father roars at her not to use that word. "Your mother was a lady. You're going to be a lady if I have to beat you black and blue to make you one." Maggie laughs, her father tries not to laugh, and suddenly you see the relationship between father and daughter.

On the first page of *Charlotte's Web* you learn a lot about Fern. Her mother tells her that her father has decided to do away with one of the new piglets, a runt. "Do away with it?" shrieked Fern. "You mean kill it? Just because it's smaller than the others?"

## Minor Characters

A really superb children's book is peopled by a gallery of live characters, and as they are involved in the action of the story, however briefly, even minor characters should emerge as personalities. At the very least there should be a little carefully constructed dialogue entwined with bits of action that give a clear impression.

Fern's brother, Avery, is first made known to readers in two all-sufficient sentences. "Avery was ten. He was heavily armed—an air rifle in one hand, a wooden dagger in the other."

Later, E. B. White employs a useful device to describe someone in a book—letting another character talk about him. Dr. Dorian asks how Avery is:

> "Oh, Avery," chuckled Mrs. Arable. "Avery is always fine. Of course, he gets into poison ivy and gets stung by wasps and bees and brings frogs and snakes home and breaks everything he lays his hands on. He's fine."

The conversation between Mrs. Arable and Dr. Dorian paints a comfortable picture of this wise and humorous country physician and elevates the doctor to a distinct personality. Very suitably, the author makes Dr. Dorian the one who perceives the miracle of Charlotte's web. No one else in this practical farming community would have interpreted the mere weaving of a spider's web as a miracle.

In *Cracker Jackson,* Cracker and his friend Goat are earning some money by raking leaves for Mrs. Marino. Mrs. Marino makes no other appearance in the book, but her repartee with the boys brightens the page and also endears Goat and Cracker to the reader:

> "I'm not paying you boys to jump up and down in leaf piles."
>
> "We're tamping them down, Mrs. Marino, so we can get more in the bags."

Five minutes later:

> "I'm not paying you boys to put each other in leaf bags."
>
> "It's a good way to open them up, Mrs. Marino."

In my book *David's Campaign Buttons,* young David is asking storekeepers to display a poster supporting his candidate in the town election, but so far no store has been willing to take one. He stops to see Mr. Greenleaf, who runs a toy shop, and tells him about it. This is Mr. Greenleaf's only appearance in the book but this bit of dialogue plus action makes him a real person:

> "They won't, eh?" The storeman stood looking at the oblong piece of cardboard. Then he marched to the front of the store, climbed into the window, set the card against the glass and backed out. "There you are." David could hardly believe it. But instead of feeling joyful he suddenly felt almost alarmed about Mr. Greenleaf. He looked up and met his friend's eyes, gazing steadily into his. "That's swell! Only, Mr. Greenleaf, I sure hope you don't

> lose any business or anything." "So I'll lose business," said Mr. Greenleaf shortly. "What am I, a mouse?"

Speech, even a child's speech, can indicate education, social background, sense of humor, and general outlook on life. You will not need to know the other people in your book as well as you know your main character, but you should have a pretty solid impression of each one.

## Handling Dialogue

Good dialogue in a book is not really true to life. In real life we repeat, stumble, put in extraneous comments. You must select in writing dialogue, just as an artist selects details in painting a portrait.

You distill out of the conglomeration of words a person would utter in real life the gist of a conversation, and you make this distillation sound completely natural. The conversation will seem much more lifelike to the reader than the mass of pointless talking we would hear if we recorded some of our actual conversations. That might not be a bad idea, for practice—record a conversation and reduce it on paper to essentials.

Dialogue is inextricably connected with action. Notice what children do as they are talking: A boy may be gobbling cookies, his face crumby, a girl patting her doll to sleep. When Maggie's father in *Me and You and a Dog Named Blue* is berating her about that report card he is leaning forward, bracing his hands on the crossbar of his crutch. He thumps his crutch on the floor. When Maggie reports that Aunt Myrt is arriving, Myrt the Squirt she calls her, he tells her to keep a civil tongue in her head and he smooths down his hair with both hands and heaves himself to his feet, leaning on his crutch. The interweaving of natural dialogue with telling action brings a character to life.

A conversation should never be tortured because you think you have to vary the "she saids." "She said" is better than some expression too obviously put in for variety. Change it only when a different verb seems called for—cried, shouted, exclaimed. And don't have someone "smile" a sentence. Make it "She smiled." Put what she said in a separate sentence.

Sometimes you can omit both the "he said" and any action. Here is an example from *Then Again Maybe I Won't* by Judy Blume. Tony is talking to the neighbor next to his stylish new home:

> "I see you're having a lot of work done on your house." "Us?" I asked. "No, we're not having anything done. It's perfect the way it is." "Well, that's funny. There's a truck parked in your driveway all the time." "Oh . . . that's my father's truck. Sometimes he drives it to work when my mother needs the car." "It belongs to your father?" "Sure. It even has his name on the door." "Oh . . . Well, thanks for helping me, Tony." "That's okay, Mrs. Hooper."

Another example of good handling of dialogue is in *Cracker Jackson* when Cracker's mother takes matters into her own hands. The author is in a hurry here and so is the reader. Alma is in danger. You want whoever is going to her to get going fast. There is clipped, rapid question-and-answer, fast forward movement.

If you omit both the "he saids" and all action, make the conversation fairly brief. A long-running dialogue can be difficult if the reader has to check back to make sure who is speaking. Also, this treatment can grow tiresome. The reader wishes the characters would stop talking and do something.

## Profanity

In many of today's books for teenagers you will find profanity, sexual references, and innuendos imbedded in the characters' talk. This could present you with a dilemma. You want to write a realistic book with relevance to today, but you do not want your book banned by a school board or a parents' group. Nor do you want it to be distasteful to yourself or to some young readers.

On the other hand, perhaps you see nothing out of order in using obscenity and sly double entendre if that's the way they talk. Realism, you say. Books that contain such talk, as well as the sexual experiences of fifteen-year-olds—not as explicit as in adult books—are on the young adult shelves of public libraries and in some school libraries too. The reasoning is, I suppose, that young people see and hear all this on TV, on video cassettes, and in movies. From thirteen on, they read uncensored contemporary adult novels.

I suspect you may find the more overt young adult books in libraries that have a generous book budget. "It's not the obscenity and sex so much," said a librarian with a tight budget. "These kids have seen the seamy side of life. I like to give them some books that show the other side." "What books, for instance?" I asked. She admitted she had to recommend some of the older books to readers.

Another factor is a Supreme Court ruling that obscenity comes down to what the local community will tolerate. If the librarian judges that the mores of the community will find a book acceptable and that the book will engender circulation she will probably buy it.

### Is Profanity in Character?

The extent to which you use profanity and obscenity depends on the characters in your book. Such talk would probably be an accurate portrayal of some seventeen-year-olds, decent enough boys, trying to appear macho. In *A*

*Solitary Blue* I doubt if you will find any bad language. Jeff is a serious boy, a quiet boy because his father rarely has anything to say to him. Painfully anxious to please his scholarly father, Jeff would never use a distasteful word.

In *The Chocolate War* Archie, arch-demon of the nefarious school organization, The Vigils, says "What the hell" and "goddam" routinely, but he does not use much profanity. When his cohort Obie calls him a bastard and "a goddam king," Archie chides, "Don't swear, Obie. You'll have to tell it in confession." Archie is bad. He is growing into an evil man. He does not need to get excited and swear, because he controls and manipulates by ruthless calculation. Archie's quiet is more sinister than the other boys' emotional epithets. This characterization has a deadly accuracy about it.

A lawsuit was brought against a library about one "Jesus Christ!" uttered by a fifteen-year-old when he discovers his leg has been amputated. The library and the judge thought the expletive justified and the book went back on the shelf.

If you are writing for teenagers but bad language offends you, experiment with tricks that will convey the flavor but avoid exact expressions. Have your hero aim a vicious kick at a tree and mutter words under his breath. Is this Victorian? Cheating? It's up to you. You must rely on your skill in dealing with words.

## In Younger Books

Profanity is absent in *Cracker Jackson,* a story of eleven-year-olds. These two, Cracker and Goat, are still little boys. Life is a hilarious joke to Goat and he shows off by boasting and being silly, not by swearing.

When the boys are actually driving a car, to take Alma to safety, Goat is nervous, quite rightly, about Cracker's driving. Another author might have given him a line with an expletive in it. But no, Cracker, exhausted by twenty minutes of driving, is only too happy to let Goat take the wheel. Goat shows himself a brilliant driver, in his own estimation, only sorry he can't tell his mom. The reader ends up breathless, the humor is intact, and Goat stays completely in character.

Nor is there youthful profanity in *Bridge to Terabithia.* If ten-year-old Jesse had used a swear word his Daddy would have licked the daylights out of him. Momma sobs, "Oh my God! Oh my God!" when Jesse, whom she has believed drowned, walks in. The words burst out of her. Momma is not swearing; she is thanking God.

Children copy their parents and older siblings. It was reported to me with amusement that a seven-year-old stormed at her parents, who were going out to dinner without her, "God! I won't put up with this!" This hardly seems serious profanity, but used in a book it might seem blasphemy to some. You could get the same effect with "I won't put up with this!"

Even words that seem innocuous to you may offend someone. A woman wrote me of one of my books that it was a nice book but ruined for her because the boy said "Gosh!"

It may be revealing for you to examine the dialogue in books on the young adult shelves, but it all goes back to that question of your own personal taste and judgment.

## *Something Else*

There is something else that may arouse the displeasure of some parents or a group and get your book banned in some state—so-called un-Americanism. An organization exists so dedicated to anti-Communism that it will finance lawsuits aimed at banning controversial books considered un-American. Or, possibly, unreligious. I offer you no advice. How strong your personal convictions may be, to right or to left, may govern your characters, their views and their talk. This could conceivably present a problem in a teenage book. It arose, innocently on my part, when a woman wrote the publisher about one of my stories that the author must be a Communist because she made Americans such fools about their pets. A remote problem, this, in juvenile books, but worth mention.

Youthful slang that has become yesterday's dates a story. My advice is to leave out current slang in a story of today when you make your characters talk; that slang may be old-hat by the time the book is published. This is easy to say but, again, if you are writing about today's young people you want them to talk the way children and teenagers do talk. Try to use slang expressions that seem perennial.

## Dialect

"Vernacular" and "dialect" are close in meaning. One definition of vernacular is "the native or indigenous language of a country or district." Dialect is "a variety of language arising from local peculiarities. A provincial method of speech."

Regional dialect must be carefully handled when you are using dialogue to delineate a character in a geographical background important to the story. The dialect must be accurate. You must know those people and how they talk, or someone is going to resent it, or it will strike a false note. Dialect will hamper your story if the reader has to slow down to understand it.

The characters in Katherine Paterson's books with Appalachian background—*Bridge to Terabithia* and *Sing, Jimmy Jo*—are the product of their environment, and their speech patterns bring color and verisimilitude to the stories. Mrs. Paterson knows the area and the people she writes about and she has the talent for putting down on paper in appealing style what her ear has recorded.

Racial dialect is even more difficult and more subject to criticism. One instance of successful dialect is in Virginia

Hamilton's *Sweet Whispers, Brother Rush.* Here the language of the black family is intriguing in itself because some of it may be new to the reader, and its use quickens interest in characters and story. There is a subtle gradation in the speech of the various characters due to exposure to the outside world.

The pages of your book would be monotone in color if every person talked like every other. We have already discussed the importance of the individual manner of speaking and what speech tells about a character. Now we are talking about getting local flavor into your dialogue when a character is identified with a region. This is one thing that cannot be dredged up from your imagination. Dialect of the area or nationality you are writing about is a subject for study.

## *Caution*

Everyone speaks with a regional inflection and uses some local verbiage. You cannot consider the accent and vernacular of the part of the country where you are writing as standard American speech and other regional talk strange and even amusing. Your book is going to be read—you hope it is—in every state, by people who use different idioms and pronunciations, and to whom your own accent would sound strange.

## *Just a Touch*

If you need to get just a touch of regional speech or a foreign accent you can do it by the way you arrange the words. Here an Italian woman is speaking in my *Libby Shadows a Lady:*

> "That policeman? Yes, perhaps. But I must collect these thoughts first. I have most terrible

> thoughts about this bomb, this kidnapping. I must manage myself, think what is reasonable to believe."

And later:

> "But," she said then, "you have these kidnappers now. Please, explain to me how this comes about."

In *Lily and the Lost Boy* by Paula Fox a native man on a Greek island is speaking English: "That boy—he run away . . ." And again, when he gives Lily a little carving: "I see you like."

When a tiny child appears in your book you can arrange words and use short sentences or half-sentences to convey the effect of baby talk.

For some beginning authors dialogue comes naturally. For others it seems to be a hard technique to master. It does not need to be. It depends on a keen ear and observing eye, and those are tools you can sharpen. Listen, on buses and everywhere, to the way people talk, especially how children talk, and accustom your ear to recording speech and the mannerisms that go with it. Jot down amusing or significant bits of speech or speech incidents. Read the conversations in *Then Again Maybe I Won't,* by Judy Blum, *It's like this, Cat,* by Emily Neville, or *Harriet the Spy* by Louise Fitzhugh. Read your own dialogue aloud. Is it natural? Right for the person talking?

## How Old Should Your Book Child Be?

The common-sense answer to the question of how old the children in a book should be, sometimes asked by new writers, is "How old must they be for the story you want to write?" That should be your only consideration.

If it would help, however, to picture the children who will read your book, advice is offered by librarians about how old juvenile readers are in relation to the characters they enjoy reading about. Children like to read, they say, about characters three years older than themselves. One librarian told me that some books that used to be read by sixth-graders are fourth-grade level now. Children are growing up faster.

It is believed that children do not like to read about a character younger than they are, but what about *A Solitary Blue,* which takes Jerry from age seven to young adulthood? I receive fan mail about my picture books from boys and girls who should have outgrown that kind of story. Also, children go back and read a favorite book over and over again when they have grown to be much older than the book characters. Publishers' classification of a juvenile as right for eight-to-twelves indicates that considerable variation among readers is expected. It depends on the mental age of the reader.

My books are about eight-to-twelves and they are read by that age group. They tell me how old they are and send me their pictures in fan mail. I have often kept a picture on my desk so I could hold in my mind the little girls I was writing about and the little girls who read my books.

So forget about age groups. Write the story you want to write about the characters, of whatever age, you want to write about, and let your story find its audience. An editor will know what audience that is.

## Will Readers Like Your Hero or Heroine?

The chief character in a children's book should be one your reader willingly identifies with. Make sure that girl in the book is not perfect. If she is too good or too smart readers will hate her; maybe they won't even read the book.

She must embody some of the human failings the reader secretly recognizes in herself, but those failings should be balanced by likable traits. The reader sees those in herself too.

You are drawn to Dave in *It's like this, Cat* right away because of his cheerful set-tos with his father. The boy reading the book identifies with Dave, and he may also see his father in Dave's father, which quickly establishes a bond.

If you make your leading character unpleasant at the start of the story, due to an unhappy or difficult situation, there should be something in the character that enables the reader to empathize. In *The Divorce Express* Phoebe does dreadful things at school, such as glueing down toilet seats and everything else glueable. The young reader may find her pranks amusing but cannot help being appalled. But the author has already explained that "something happened" to Phoebe after her parents' divorce, so the reader is willing to withhold judgment of her outrageous conduct, to wait and see.

In a story that shows character development, some less-than-admirable quality in hero or heroine will give way as the story progresses, and the reader will rejoice in tribulation overcome and the emergence of good qualities that were there, latent, all the time. Girl readers will approve Phoebe's affection for Rocky the raccoon, and this will offset that business at school.

How to show change and growth in your character will take a lot of thought. You must know that child in the book so well that you can predict what the reaction to a situation will be and make change believable. Change must come not in one big rush but in step-by-step development.

You might examine *The Pinballs* for the skillful and sensitive way in which Betsy Byars shows fifteen-year-old Carlie's development. At the start Carlie is hard, tough, suspicious, and rude. She's a dreadful child. But the reader knows her background, so she is also a pitiable child. In little, grudging, almost imperceptible steps Carlie changes, the reader feeling and moving right along with her. At the end of the book she is still Carlie, but a softer Carlie whose bitter outlook has changed. The reader knows Carlie will be all right now.

## Names for Your Characters

The children's names in your book should appeal to the readers. To find the right name for a character you might go down the pages of a telephone book or scan articles in a newspaper until you chance on a name that seems just right for your boy or girl. A good solid boy deserves to be Henry, Samuel, John. A diminutive, for a girl, makes girl readers feel she is a friend, and a striking and unusual name lifts that girl out of the ordinary. Try an amusing nickname for a boy, especially if it says something about him or has a funny origin. Surnames, too, can be found in a newspaper or a telephone book.

Now we must turn our attention to that all-important strength of a book that we mentioned briefly at the start—the story itself, the conflict.

# 5

# The Conflict Is the Story

Before I began to write this chapter I read my earlier chapters. Suddenly I wanted to shout at beginning writers, "*Don't* visit the juvenile shelves in the library. *Don't* read other modern writers. It will only confuse you. It may discourage you."

Then reason began to prevail. I pictured the readers of my book in two groups. Some of you may already be writing for children. You have had small successes, but you have written a book and it's made the rounds and you haven't sold it. You have decided, reluctantly because you are suspicious of instruction and writing by rules, that perhaps you could use a little help.

Others of you long to write for children and you have a story in mind, but you don't know how to get started.

Some of you have writing in your genes. My own writing genes have trailed down through a couple of centuries. When I began to write for children I did not study contemporary juvenile authors; I didn't even know who they were. I could put pretty or amusing words on paper, but that wasn't enough. I needed a lot of help along the way from a teacher and from editors, on the techniques of writing a book for children.

If your genes are not primarily writing genes, or even if they are, it will do you no harm to visit those shelves and see what published authors are writing for children. It would be helpful for you to read the authors I quote in this volume. Think about how your style and the kind of book you are writing compare with their work.

Then go home, inspired by some books you have looked at, envious of others, maybe disgusted by a few and wondering how they ever got published. Shut those books out of your mind and write your own kind of story. Using every technique you can learn and master, and with love of words leading the way, work, study, revise to make it a better book!

Now let's move on to the substance of your book, the conflict. Call it the plot if you prefer, the story line, story pattern, main line, or just the story. In fiction, conflict is a technical term that means the play of opposing forces. It is the ups and downs of the situation, the problem you are writing about, which your child characters and your readers are going to move through and survive. It can apply to a story of exciting adventure or it can be softened, in a simple tale, to a point where the reader is hardly aware any conflict is taking place.

If a little girl walks down the street in an April shower and sees some daffodils, there is no conflict and no story. Perhaps a poem. If the gutter is running with rain water and she can't resist walking in the water, and her new umbrella gets away and she goes home soaking wet when Mother has told her not to play in puddles, we have several conflicts. Is she or isn't she going to walk in the water when she knows she shouldn't? How will she explain to Mother? Mother has a conflict too—how to handle the disobedience.

This might make an incident in a juvenile story. It might even make a book if the disobedience were part of a pattern of disobedience and defiance. The author could seek out reasons for the chronic disobedience and start that little girl on the process of working out some problem.

A good story requires conflict that an author, like this hypothetical author, has elevated to importance. The conflict in a juvenile story takes place among children, and the problems and their solutions should stay in the province of children. The conflict should present some hard choices the book character must make in solving the problem, and on the decisions should hang grief or joy. That is your story.

Children face some of the same situations, feel the same emotions, as adults. The difference between a juvenile and an adult novel is that situations are less complex. Some psychological development should take place in a way with which child readers can identify.

There will be grown-ups in your book, but unless the parents are an important part of the problem they should be there as they are in a real child's world, supportive or exasperating and usually loving people who are taken for granted; who provide necessary service and must be allowed for and dealt with. They may offer advice, do what they can to help, but a parent should never become a deus ex machina.

The way the boy or girl in your book works out the problem makes your story. Carlie in *The Pinballs* fights her own hard way through her troubles even though kind adults stand longing to help. Cathy in my *Cathy Leonard Calling* makes her own decision to stop being that world wonder, a ten-year-old newspaper reporter; no parent orders her to stop.

In *Ginnie and Geneva* I see now that I broke this rule. Ginnie has finally adjusted to her new environment. She has friends, she has learned to ice-skate. She loves school. She is happy. Then the blow strikes. She must leave all this, go away to her grandmother's gloomy house. It is not really Ginnie who saves the day; her friends do. But, at least, two of the friends are other girls, and the two women have legitimate reasons for intervening on Ginnie's behalf.

Why didn't I have Ginnie just tell her mother flatly that she didn't want to go? Because the approach I did take made a better story. Be pragmatic. Always consider the story and complications that will make it a better story.

It is all right to let your child turn to a parent in desperation if the problem has proved more than a child can realistically be expected to handle. In *Cracker Jackson* Cracker finally confides in his mother; he is frightened out of his wits for Alma and has no idea what to do.

You could, instead of pulling in a little adult help in a terrible situation, conceive of a tour de force by which a child achieves some unnatural triumph. Readers would love it.

Another important point: No new character or fact should be introduced at the last moment to solve the problem. All the elements in the solution should be present in the story earlier, so the reader will find the ending plausible. You may introduce an incident or remark or hint early and play it down, so the reader forgets about it, and bring it in again at the end. This is the clue, in mysteries, that the reader fails to catch.

This device can be used in other than mysteries. In *The Pinballs* Carlie remarks that the only good books are about nurses. Several times she mentions nurse books. At the end, when she decides she wants to go to nursing school, this is not an uncharacteristic surprise thrown at the reader but a reasonable development for which the author has laid the way.

In *The Pinballs* an all-important Harvey clue is dropped in too. Harvey makes a list of his Disappointments, chief among them that he never had a puppy. The reader may forget this but Carlie remembers, and finding a puppy for Harvey finally gives him something to live for.

## Your Synopsis

All right, you think you have a story. You have lots of bits and pieces in mind. To get your story organized, a good way is to do a one-page single-spaced synopsis of each chapter as you see your book divided. Gather your fragments, putting in all the detailed action you can in advance of the actual writing of the book. This synopsis will be a concise account of the story you have to tell but without dialogue or the specific scenes that we shall discuss shortly.

It must indicate the nature of the conflict your character faces. You may revise the action during the writing of the book, but you will have an outline to guide you.

In writing your synopsis you must decide on the time frame for your story. A juvenile book can take place in a few days, weeks or months, even years, whichever seems right for the purpose you wish to accomplish. The younger the reading audience you envision, the shorter the time frame as well as the book itself should be.

As you write the synopsis and then read it through, you should be able to see certain techniques that you will employ as you expand your synopsis into the manuscript of a book. What are these techniques?

## The Beginning

The start of your book should orient the reader by giving him certain information. It should spotlight the main character. It should make clear where the action is taking place, and when. Here is the first line of *Then Again Maybe I Won't:* "Who says March is supposed to . . . go out like a lamb?" The next two paragraphs show a boy named Tony tossing a newspaper onto Mrs. Gorsky's porch—a *Jersey Journal,* so you know Tony lives in New Jersey. His approximate age is indicated by the fact that he is a paperboy.

In *A Solitary Blue* the first paragraph shows Jeff, seven-and-a-half, coming home from school to an empty house on a Tuesday in early March, and finding a note from his mother saying she has gone away and will not be coming back. Page two shows Jeff frightened and crying, but knowing he must stop because his father the Professor doesn't like crying. You have characters and a situation. Where the home is is not important at the moment.

Both beginnings strike a spark of interest in the young reader who is deciding whether or not to read the book.

The nature of the basic conflict—what the story will be about—should become clear, or at least the reader should be given a clue, in the first chapter. We are talking about an eight-to-twelve book or a young adult novel. The special requirements of picture books for very young children will be discussed later.

Keep in mind as you write that child readers need things clearly explained. They are not geared to understanding an innuendo. For very bright readers not everything needs to be spelled out, but you cannot assume that the average reader will understand subtle undertones.

## *Happy or Unhappy Start?*

A story may begin with a happy situation. Is the child's happiness due to family? Place? Friends? What would happen if his or her mother were taken away or the child had to move to a strange place?

*Then Again Maybe I Won't* begins with a good situation. Tony lives in Jersey City with his family, a grandma who cooks delicious meals, his paper route, baseball, and pals. He is content. An upturn in family fortunes and a move to Long Island change all this and Tony looks at prosperity with a jaundiced eye.

The author's thinking may start with a sad situation. In *A Solitary Blue,* as we have seen, the story begins with Jeff's weeping at his mother's desertion. The reader will identify if a story strikes home; he or she has endured unhappiness. Emotions involved, readers will be deeply stirred. They may cry and even enjoy crying. If a story does begin on a note of unhappiness or alarm, the characters in the course of the story must make their way through to some acceptable resolution.

## Action at the Start

Action right at the start will give your book a lively send-off. Dialogue can be used in the first sentence; something a character says and how it is said can present an instant image, as it does in *Me and You and a Dog Named Blue* and *Then Again Maybe I Won't.* Action, dialogue, or a combination can imply the nature of the story to come.

*Charlotte's Web,* that finest of children's books, begins with action, dialogue, and setting. The first page tells the reader that a family is involved, the setting is a farm, a little girl named Fern is the chief character, and a newly born piglet is a runt that Fern is determined to save.

It is important not to open your story with lengthy exposition. Both editor and reader will decide after looking at your first page whether to read on. An experienced editor can tell a great deal about a manuscript from the first two pages, and if interest is not engaged right away the reading may never go further.

There are exceptions to the no-exposition-at-the-start rule. In *The Pinballs* a brief expository chapter opens the book, to explain the backgrounds of the three children and why each is going to a foster home. But this exposition is lightened with action and dialogue. There are four pages of exposition at the start of *A Solitary Blue,* but the reader is caught up by that note from Jeff's mother in the first paragraph and must read on to find out what is going to happen.

But as a rule a child may put a book right back on the library shelf if it starts with a solid block of type and nothing happening. He will look for a book with more talking.

A sometimes useful technique is the flashback after a dramatic opening. In *So Far From the Bamboo Grove* Yoko Watkins starts her story in striking fashion:

> It was almost midnight on July 29, 1945, when my mother, my elder sister Ko, and I, carrying as many of our belongings as we could on our

> backs, fled our home in its bamboo grove, our friends, and our town, Nanam, in northern Korea, forever.

She has action, actors, and a setting. But once she has engaged the reader's interest she must explain why they are leaving, so she uses the flashback. For twenty pages she tells why this Japanese family was living in North Korea, about her family and happy home, how the shadow of war had crept up, and why they were now in such peril they must flee. Then she picks up from where she started, and in chapter two the gripping story goes on. Had she begun with a long account of her childhood in Korea she could have lost the reader at the start.

## The Middle

In writing your synopsis you indicate in detail the action that takes place in each chapter. When you start to translate synopsis into full-sized book you will begin to move your story forward by writing scenes made up of action and dialogue, in good balance, each scene representing a further step in the story. A scene may be only a few lines, or it may last for several pages. You decide as you write how much time and wordage your scene requires.

You will connect these scenes with a little exposition, useful for telescoping a period of time and some not too important action into a few paragraphs. The important thing is to shift from a close-up scene—action taking place right before the reader's eyes—to a long shot, which is exposition.

You must have this alternation of sharply delineated scenes and the links of more remote exposition not only to progress from scene to scene and move the story on in time, but also because readers cannot take an unbroken succession of close-up scenes. They need to relax in between. But these breathing spells between scenes would become dull and the story would fall flat if you used too much exposition and did not put in another close-up soon.

Every author has an individual style. Some books, such as *The Pinballs,* have page after page airy with dialogue—important dialogue that carries the story on. Sometimes you have to search the lines to find the bits of exposition that are skillfully built in. *A Solitary Blue* presents pages of solid-looking exposition, but in those pages what the author is telling is so fascinating that the reader forgets he is reading exposition.

As you gain proficiency you will develop a sense of timing—when to shift from scene to exposition and how long each should be. You will also discover a natural writing style of your own.

It is important to build up to the climax in a scene, if a climax is called for, at the right tempo. This may take practice and rewriting, but you will come to sense the need to hold some scene, especially at the high point in your story, a little longer, so that you fully involve the emotions of your reader. The reader does not want to be dragged away from the action too soon, but he will welcome a release from tension at the right moment. You will come to sense when that moment arrives. Then he does not want the author to explain for too long before getting to the next absorbing scene of action.

Action and dialogue in a scene must be well balanced. A character should not go on talking too long, and some action should accompany the talk. Dialogue and action should have relevance to the story and move it along. No idle chitchat. A character's announcement of what he is about to do, a mere hint, can leave the reader looking ahead with eager anticipation.

In developing your conflict, dialogue can be used instead of exposition to convey information, but you must learn to handle this technique well or it can sound like a speech. If you make someone talk to tell another person in the book, and the reader, something they need to know, instead of telling the reader yourself through exposition, be sure the talk is natural. Break up big chunks of dialogue, let your speaker breathe and move, others respond.

You move your story along by means of alternating scenes and exposition. You drop in a new complication, perhaps another essential character. You show progress your chief character is making, offset by defeat, then more progress and another setback. The tension builds. You keep the reader always wondering what will happen next.

Entwined with your major line of action, at least one subplot, which can be a slim one, should be introduced. In *Ginnie and the New Girl* Ginnie loses her pal Geneva to a new girl in town. In the end Geneva becomes her best friend again but, as a subplot, changes are promised in the lonely life of the third girl. In *Ginnie and the Mystery Doll* the mystery of the ancient doll is solved and in the process a poor and embittered boy is promised a chance to go to college.

You will need lots of minor incidents that fill out the story, but these small events must be made to have relevance. A notebook in which you jot down small occurrences is useful.

Through all of this you must hold to the conflict you established in your synopsis. Is the conflict between two characters? Be sure it stays that way. Is it an inner struggle between two opposing traits in your main character? Often it is both, because these are not separate techniques. The juvenile *Understood Betsy* is a perfect example. A little girl, pampered into believing herself frail, is put into a farm family where she is expected to pull her weight. The battle rages within herself, but there are other people to deal with. Gradually she adjusts and emerges as a new child. This is a simply told tale but a full-fledged psychological novel.

Keep clear in your mind where the conflict lies, and check to be sure you have not strayed.

Chapter breaks are important. If one chapter has ended with climactic action you may need a bit of expository writing, just a touch, to start the next chapter. This will give the reader time for a breath. Examine *Charlotte's Web* and you will see that almost every chapter starts with brief exposition, and often the exposition indicates a passage of time. This is also true of *Ginnie and Geneva.* An important device, this, to move your story along.

The end of a chapter must always leave the reader avid to go on. This is the secret of keeping your young reader wanting "just one more chapter, please!"

One thing to remember as you plan your book and write it is that you are the all-powerful author. As long as what you are making your people do is reasonable, you can make anything happen. If your story is based on actual events or real people, there is a pull toward limiting yourself to what happened in real life. That may not be interesting enough or it may not be convenient for the purpose of your fictional story. Don't be trapped by reality. Break out of it when necessary into fresh fictional events that will appear completely real to your reader.

## Put Your Character Where the Action Is

An important principle must be considered in working out your action. You are going to adhere strictly to the technique of the single viewpoint that we discussed in the previous chapter. You are going to make certain that all is experienced from the viewpoint of your chief character, so you must put your character on the spot when something happens. In your own life events are more interesting, exciting, and important when you experience them firsthand. They are never as sharp when they happen to someone else or in a different place and someone relays the news to you. The instinct to be there, not wait to hear about it, sends people flocking to watch a fire destroy a house.

Tying the child in the book directly to all the action sometimes requires considerable ingenuity. It may take some juggling of time and place, and perhaps of fact too if the story is based on reality, to bring all the action into the purview of the main character.

This is a challenge. It can also be fun, like working out a jigsaw puzzle, and the skill and imagination with which you manipulate your material will determine the immediacy of the narrative and your success as an author.

In *Cracker Jackson* Cracker's mother goes swooping out in her car and Cracker knows she is going to Alma's. He could have waited at home and his mother could eventually have come back and told him that Alma's husband had beaten her and the baby so severely that she has taken them to the hospital. This would have been secondhand information. In the book, Cracker leaps onto his bicycle, follows his mother, and sees for himself the wreck Billy Ray has made of Alma's treasured possessions. He heads for the hospital. He missed the struggle between Alma and Billy Ray, but that might have been too much in a children's book.

To sum this up: Don't use clichés such as "Meanwhile in a house down the road . . ." Take the main character down the road or move the action up the road to your character.

There is a special suspense technique that seems to defy the rule of the single viewpoint. The author may shift the story back and forth between two characters or two lines of action that are going to converge.

But you can use this technique and still keep to the viewpoint of one character. When you shift to what the other is doing just show what that character is doing; don't tell what is going on inside his or her head.

Even this rule, however, is broken with success in *So Far From the Bamboo Grove.* The action alternates between the heroine, making her way out of the dangers of North Korea at the end of World War II, and her brother, following his own lonely path to find his family. Here you have two good people, not adversaries, and because you want so much to see them united you can identify easily with the emotions of both.

## The Ending

The ups and downs in your story have soared to a climax. Your characters have worked out their problems and the story is finished. Wind it up quickly. It is important to avoid any anticlimax following the high point, so the young reader will close the book at the peak of interest with a sigh of satisfaction.

The subplot should be tied in with the ending. In *A Room for Cathy,* Cathy at the start achieves her heart's desire, a room of her own. But not far into the story she has to give up her room, her precious privacy. The story works its way to the point where Cathy has adjusted. Final excitement comes fast—the great news that the room will be hers again, hers alone. There is a moment, however, when calamity hangs in the balance for another girl, whose happiness has also become important to the reader. It is Cathy's growth as a person, her quick perception and decision, that avert that personal tragedy for her friend.

In contemporary young adult books the ending is often not so much a solution of problems as a facing up to them. No teenage girl in a book who has suffered from her parents' divorce, a death, or some other traumatic experience will believe you if you tell her at the end of the book that she will live happily forever after. Nor will your reader believe it. Children learn about life early these days, and remember always that your story and how it ends must be accepted by readers. *The Great Gilly Hopkins* by Katherine Paterson, for subteens, is another story about a fighting foster child. At the end Gilly and her foster mother, both grieving at their separation, know a chapter in Gilly's life has ended and she must move on.

The happy ending is traditional in stories for young children and I hope you will hold to it. Let a little girl or boy be happy, lost in your book. If a young reader has already been hurt by life, help that child escape for a while. Children will love your book and ask for it over and over. It may become part of a life.

In a story of mystery or adventure you may, if you wish, solve the problem in the next to last chapter or the first part of the final chapter. The last pages can be devoted to a discussion by the chief players, a review and analysis of events that have taken place. If unsure about some detail, now the reader will understand. I did this in *Ginnie and the Mystery Doll.*

## Mysteries

Mysteries for young children are sometimes a kind of parody of adult books. There is young Roger Teale, known as the Inspector, in Scott Corbett's *The Case of the Silver Skull.* The Inspector has a voracious appetite for catching criminals and in the end he actually catches one and proves smarter than the police. A junior mystery should be suspenseful but amusing—to the reader if not to the juvenile detective—and if you make the denouement a triumph for your sleuth you will delight your readers.

There are variations of the true mystery plot. In *The Lancelot Closes at Five* by Marjorie Weinman Sharmat, Hutch devises her own mystery and succeeds in baffling the police and everyone else, but the case has consequences she hadn't anticipated. The ending is funny and wonderful. Readers will gasp with dismay and chortle with laughter at the same time.

*Harriet the Spy* sounds like a mystery but it's just a little girl with a notebook peeking in windows and peering down skylights.

In my own books the mysteries grow out of some actual occurrence, and are puzzling enough to intrigue the adults in the book. What is the secret of the old lady's weird house? Of the beautiful antique doll? What is that mysterious light? Who was the nighttime intruder? Is the attractive young woman really going to bomb the Federal Reserve Bank? But the adults would not bother to become involved were it not for the girl sleuth, who pulls others into helping her get the answer but remains the moving force.

For teenage readers, Betty Cavanna has done many mysteries with intriguing foreign backgrounds. *Mystery on Safari* is laid in Kenya, about a young girl on safari who becomes involved in the pursuit and capture of a poaching combine. In a teenage mystery you will drop clues along the way, which your young detective picks up. You work up to an exciting climax in which your sleuth takes part, you catch the criminals, and at the end lay out the whole exploit, which may have become so involved that the reader needs things explained.

There is no discernible character development in mystery stories but in mine there is a character trait that carries every story to its solution—the heroine's unflagging determination to get to the bottom of things. In *Cathy Uncovers a Secret* Cathy learns a lot as step by step she unravels her mystery; this can be considered growth. Grown-ups usually have to help a little at some point, in junior mysteries, if the stories are to be believable.

Conflict is the most difficult of all writing techniques to teach, to learn, and to put into practice. There is no rigid pattern for your juvenile novel. You need the right proportion of ups and downs, the ups getting higher and downs deeper as your story progresses. Sometimes the ups will come crashing down, sometimes the downs soar. The right tempo is essential. This will take practice, a lot of writing and thought and rewriting. But the skill will come if you really work at it.

## Humor

Before ending the discussion of conflict, that important element, humor, should be considered. I mentioned it in the chapter on ideas. Humor should be woven into your story if at all possible.

For older children anything that would be funny to them in real life can be counted on to be funny in a book. Children love a little horseplay. They like corny jokes, roughhouse, and silly carryings-on. These things don't have to be funny to adults, because adults don't read the books.

There is a different kind of humor, one more closely knit into your story and made to move it along—humor based on a situation. This humor appeals to every age from youngest to grown-ups. A little boy feels too sick to go to school until he remembers today is Saturday. Cathy sets her alarm wrong and gets breakfast at two A.M. Mr. Porter, in *Ginnie and Geneva,* mutters about those kittens, they've got to go, and then is discovered by the girls secretly warming milk for the mother cat.

This is humor with a human quality and endears the characters to the reader. The girl reading the book may not laugh out loud as she will at comic antics, but she may giggle a bit and she will feel good, not only because the story is funny but because she feels superior to those silly people. When a story seems flat as you write it, very likely it is not one bit funny.

Humor can make a sad or serious story easier to enjoy. Bitter, suspicious Carlie in *The Pinballs,* with her telling retorts, makes the story heartbreakingly funny too. Her new foster mother puts a hand on her shoulder and Carlie, absorbed in a TV show, jerks away. "I just wanted to welcome you." "Welcome me during the commercial."

Take *Anne of Green Gables,* by L. M. Montgomery. At the beginning especially this is a serious book. A girl's happiness, her future, are at stake. But the story is filled with gentle humor. All along the line we laugh at Anne. We laugh and we cry.

When someone says, "I loved that book!" the chances are there was laughter in the book. Probably there was pathos too. When you have made your reader laugh and cry over your book, you have scored a success.

## If You Get Off the Track

As an author writing a story you must know where you want to go in your book and have the single-mindedness to get there via a plenitude of action. Your mind will wander, refuse to concentrate all its powers and shy away from the straight line. One way to get back on the track is to ask yourself some questions, your manuscript before you:

1. Do I make clear very early who the chief character is, where the action is taking place, and the nature of the story to come?
2. Do I catch my reader's interest at once?
3. Do I keep to a single viewpoint?
4. Do I tell the story through scenes of action and dialogue, with a skillful and minimal blend of exposition?
5. Is there enough action or is the story thin?
6. Does the action grow steadily in interest to a climax and turning point?
7. Does my character grow in some way and is that growth believable?
8. Are there some subplots or minor action that tie in with the main plot?
9. Have I put in any extraneous action or characters I don't need?
10. Is my ending plausible, without anticlimax and without any new element, and does it tie up all loose ends?

Books for very small children require a different approach from the older stories we have been discussing, and you may well have that kind of book in mind as you contemplate a writing career. We go on to that important area of children's literature, the picture book.

# 6

# *For the Very Young*

It was a Sunday afternoon and I was four years old. I sat on my mother's lap in a rocking chair that I still have and she read me *The Wizard of Oz.* At the end of every chapter she said hopefully, "That's enough for now," but I wouldn't let her stop. It was dark and she was so hoarse she could barely speak when she finished the book. I sighed deeply and said, "Read it again."

My father was always bringing books home to me. I still have *The Three Bears* and *Adventures of a Brownie.* They bear just the illustrator's name and they were part of a series that the publisher called *Children's Stories That Never Grow Old.*

A story for small children perhaps has a better chance than an older book never to grow old because it need not become involved in contemporary settings and mores. But a picture book, however simple, will be better for having the kind of recognizable theme—not consciously detectable to the author or to a child—that I have discussed. This is what makes a story survive. A story about a cat that insists on eating dinner on the table will be smiled at by cat lovers for its cattishness. Everyone will recognize a little boy with imaginary friends. Later I shall discuss some books that tap deeply into a child's frustrations and waking dreams.

Here Jane Thayer enters the picture. Early in my career, when I was about to have a picture book published by William Morrow and Company for the first time, my editor asked me to adopt a second name. I was producing too many books, she said, to publish under one name. That year there would be four books. I chose my grandmother's name and Jane Thayer became the author of all my picture books. My present editor and I decided that Jane's name should be on the cover of this volume because she is known to such a large audience of readers.

Books for the very, very young are picture books, in which story and pictures share space. A picture book may be a hundred words long, three hundred, or a thousand. It may be the simplest *I Can Read* book with large type and wide spacing. It may turn into a solid story with action, characters, and dialogue.

To decide whether an idea is good picture book material, look for an illustration in every three or four sentences. If there is action in your story strong enough for a book, you will see the pictures. Without picture possibilities but with an entertaining idea you might have a story for a juvenile magazine.

## Is There Humor in Your Book?

When I think of a picture book I think of a story children will love to laugh at or laugh with. Let's examine the concept of humor. I saw a definition that impressed me and I do not know who gave it: "Humor is an acceptance of life."

The most delightful adults I know are those who accept, with grace and amused resignation, both the minor tribulations that beset us all and the seemingly unexplainable things that happen. The bores are the ones who reject life as being, on the whole, outrageous. This conception of humor can quite usefully be kept in mind when writing for children.

Think about it in connection with what goes on in young children's books. A little boy says, "There's a lion under the table." If his mother says, "Don't be silly," she has wiped out the fun and the humor with three words and she may have a sullen child on her hands.

If she says, "How are you, Mr. Lion?" they are off to a rollicking bit of nonsense that children will love. Mother has accepted the lion. A child says, "I saw a horse and he said . . ." and again you have the makings of humor. Unless Mother says, "You know horses can't talk." In a good picture book with this kind of nonsense, you will see that mother cooperates!

Here are several situations that can be counted on to produce amusement in books for young children:

1. Deadpan seriousness of the characters in accepting the ridiculous. A little boy floats up to the ceiling because he is holding a bunch of balloons.
2. Amusing resignation of characters in accepting what is presented as the inevitable. A little boy has to sleep on the floor because his imaginary friends take up all the bed.
3. A topsy-turvy situation. A puppy wants a boy.
4. Animals outwitting people. A cat wangles himself into a home.
5. Children outwitting grown-ups in innocent ways. A little girl fools her mother.
6. Children or animals triumphant in a situation in which they would not normally triumph. A little boy knows how to stop a runaway horse.
7. A situation obviously imaginary and whimsical but perfectly logical within its own frame of reference once the premise is accepted by the reader. A book about a ghost falls in this category.

## *A Chuckling Reaction*

In a book which parents are going to read aloud, the humor, although childlike, should get a chuckling reaction from the parents, or they won't be able to endure reading it over and over. Children want a favorite read over and over forever.

Another source of humor lies in words and word patterns. A word pattern can be amusing in itself and not for anything it says. Certain repetitions, arrangements. Think of Kipling's "great grey green greasy Limpopo River, all set about with fever trees." His elephant child's "satiable curtiosity." The term "elephant child" itself. Much more amusing than "a little elephant."

## If an Animal Is the Hero

An animal is often the main character in a picture book. Little children take animals seriously as people and sometimes you can use an animal to get an idea across where you could not use a human. In a story of mine called *Mrs. Hen's Vacation,* Mrs. Hen went off for a few days' rest but couldn't wait to get home to her chicks. If the character had been a human mother this probably would have been an adult story.

In spite of this example to the contrary, try not to give your animal human characteristics. Find out what a squirrel might do that is true to squirrel nature, what a squirrel's problems might be. Your squirrel will talk, but have him say things you believe he might say if he could speak English. Give your animal character a natural setting. In my *Where Is Squirrel?* Squirrel has gone off to a neighbor's bird feeder which is stocked with seed in summer as well as in winter.

## Fantasy Has Its Logic

Animal heroes bring us to the subject of fantasy because many stories about animals for young children have the animals doing fantastic things.

When someone says, "I'd like to write for children," he or she is usually thinking of a fantastical tale. You yourself may very well be in this group. Many beginning writers try fantasy, probably because they think anything can happen. This is not true.

I described one humorous situation as "obviously imaginary and whimsical but perfectly logical within its own frame of reference once the premise is accepted."

If you start with a real animal doing animal things, such as a squirrel almost flying from tree to tree, as squirrels do, and then make her learn really to fly, you have leapt with the squirrel into fantasy land. To make a good story you might give your squirrel all sorts of experiences, falling out of trees, landing on a bird feeder, and stopping for a snack. You could have her persist in spite of bumps and bruises and finally fly away. "Good-by, good-by." You might send her to some magic place for flying squirrels only.

A father said to me, "Mary Anne is crazy about dinosaurs. She dreams one might be left somewhere and she'll find it."

I took it from there. Every child knows that dinosaurs once roamed the earth, and others might share that dream with Mary Anne. Suppose the dream came true, I thought. It won't, but just suppose, children are good at that. What would happen to Mary Anne and her dinosaur? I reasoned it out in a crazy kind of logic, envisioning the problems, and wrote *Quiet on Account of Dinosaur*.

I started the same process—working from the fact that my cat was agile enough in getting up a tree but needed a rescue squad to get down and wrote *The Pussy Who Went to the Moon*.

The same sort of reasoning led to *Curious Furious Chipmunk*. I'm not sure how much of this story is fantasy. When people put out food and the chipmunk has a bonanza, that is not fantasy. Hunting season starts and all the animals except Chipmunk crawl into hiding places. No fantasy. When a sign "No Hunting on These Premises" goes up, that is real. When Chipmunk rushes off to tell his animal friends it is safe to return, is that fantasy? I don't know. Animals communicate with one another, though not in the English language. Here you may be brushing your story with a touch of fantasy.

Don't worry about whether a story you have in mind is fantasy, part fantasy, or reality. Just see that it has its own logic and consistency of character and action.

Even a genius, such as E. B. White, can usually be counted on to follow the rules of fantasy. The setting in *Charlotte's Web,* a barn, is right for his characters. He makes his animals talk to one another, but who knows what goes on among animals?.

His animals stay in character. Templeton the rat keeps his nasty nature straight through. Wilbur the pig loves mud and manure and slops and the barn and his familiar barnyard neighbors. He stays piglike. His friendship with Charlotte the spider may be stretching reality but there is a certain logic about it.

As for Charlotte, Dr. Dorian in the book remarks that if Charlotte, untaught by any mother, knows how to spin a web, isn't it just an extension of that miracle when she weaves words into the web? This is the essence of fantasy—extending reality into make-believe but keeping the consistency.

## *Ghosts and Elves*

Once you step over the line and make a ghost or an elf your hero, you are writing pure fantasy. Here is where you and your reader have a tacit agreement that there aren't really any elves, but if there were an elf he might encounter the problem the elf in your story encounters. Children pretend in their play all the time, they invent imaginary friends, and they will have no difficulty extending pretense to your book as long as you tell them a good story. "The willing suspension of disbelief," Samuel Coleridge called it.

## Editors Know

Be warned that editors and critics are quite aware of the rules. One author received a letter from her editor: "This story breaks more of the rules of fantasy than any story that's come down the pike in years."

And I saw a review of two books that said, "Both authors appear to have forgotten that fantasy has its own logic and consistency, which will not bear violation."

If you have a special flare for whimsy and humor, and delight in childlike make-believe, if you can treat your fantasy characters with lighthearted seriousness and respect, fantasy may be the field in which to concentrate your efforts and perfect your expertise. When so many miracles have become everyday occurrences, when the magic carpet has turned into a real trip to the moon and Dorothy's magic mirror in *The Wizard of Oz* is television, it seems important to keep alive a sense of wonder and an acceptance of the unexplainable.

## A Dream Is Not a Dream

There are outstanding picture books quite different from the little animal, ghost, and elf fantasies I have been describing, and they too are fantasy. *The Polar Express,* written and illustrated by Chris Allsburg, is sheer small-child fantasy, dreamy and snowy with pictures of Christmas Eve. Children travel to the North Pole to visit Santa Claus. The book has the same magic quality as *The Wizard of Oz*—it takes a real child into an unreal world.

Maurice Sendak's *Where the Wild Things Are* may seem grotesque to adults in its wild animal imagery, but children adore it. Sent to bed for misbehaving, Max takes complete control of the wild things. He tames them with BE STILL, becomes their king, and sails away home when he smells something good to eat. Max can't control his parents, but how he controls those wild things! The text, one to three lines to a page, sometimes two words, is wonderfully matter-of-fact and childlike. Here in simplest form is a mastery of lyrical language.

I suggest that you do look over picture books in your library. Study the difference between prosaic writing, acceptable enough for publication, and Maurice Sendak.

Both *The Polar Express* and *Where the Wild Things Are* will be interpreted by adults as dreams, but the authors never say they are dreams. When *The Wizard of Oz* was made into a movie they made Dorothy's great adventure a dream. My sister, mother of children, said indignantly, "It was not a dream!" Of course it wasn't, in the book. There are many editions of Oz now, but I wonder how many children have read the original book or know Oz at all except for TV. Not great writing but marvelous magic that sends a child reader soaring through space to a delectable land.

As we see in *Charlotte's Web* and *The Wizard of Oz,* picture books have no monopoly on fantasy. *Mary Poppins* is another classic. For older children there are Natalie Babbitt's *Tuck Everlasting* and the C. S. Lewis stories.

The kind of genius that created these books could be lurking in your own subconscious. Learn how to draw it out and give it expression.

## Realistic Picture Books

Leaving fantasy, you will find many picture books that are realistic and written out of personal experience.

Jane Yolen's lovely *Owl Moon* is not a story in the sense of having a plot. This book is a gentle, rhythmic account of a little girl and her father, on a night deep in snow and bright with moonlight, exchanging whoo-whoos with an owl in the woods. Illustrations can make or break a book, and these are perfect. The book came from owling experience in the author's family.

*Make Way for Ducklings* by Robert McCloskey, a classic now, came from seeing the dauntless parade of Mrs. Mallard and her ducklings through Boston traffic to an island in the Public Garden. Simple, economical lines tell the story, often in one, two, or three lines to a page. The pictures, large, realistic views of Boston with ducklings marching through, are in soft black and white and succeed in making an individual of every duckling. Mr. McCloskey drew the pictures. If you are a professional artist as well as an author, you possess a great advantage: You know just what your characters and background should look like.

As a rule, the publisher's art department will select an artist for your book, and the artist's conception and yours can be quite different. As you begin to have books published, try and get your editor to help you establish an author-artist relationship in which the artist is simpatico.

## Concept Books

There is a category of books for young children known as concept books. A concept book addresses some definite purpose or some childhood problem, and it may have a slight fictional structure, skirting the line between fiction and nonfiction.

Alvin Tresselt's *White Snow, Bright Snow* and *Hide and Seek Fog* typify one type of concept book. They arouse a child's awareness of beauty. *The Country Noisy Book* and other *Noisy* books, by Margaret Wise Brown, sharpen the sense of hearing.

Some concept books are notable for their beauty of language and image, some for the help they can give children in a traumatic situation. Perhaps there is a death in the family. Or parents have divorced. A stepparent enters the picture. Grandma must go to a nursing home. Putting on glasses for the first time or having to use a hearing aid may cause a child acute embarrassment. I think of Norma Simon's books, such as *Why Am I Different?* Teachers in elementary schools find that many of their pupils have home-based problems that affect personality and grades, and concept books can be helpful. They offer no perfect answers but they can help a child to adjust.

A book introducing a child to animals or nature or the alphabet is a concept book. I wrote a non-ABC book when a teacher told me children do not become familiar with the letters of the alphabet in ABC order.

I suggest to you still another type of concept book, one dealing with an abstract idea. I once considered doing a book about zero, a concept often hard for a small learner to grasp, but my editor did not see a sales potential. Should you be intrigued by this kind of book, your problem would be to devise a clever, clear presentation that would amuse and interest a small child, and then to find an editor who was also interested and amused and believed your book would find a market.

Ideas for concept books come from everyday life. A friend told me she had bitterly resented, as a child, having to wear her sister's out-grown clothes. Certainly a common problem and a reasonable topic for a little book. A vague old lady, told that her husband would be back soon, asked, "How long is soon?" A concept book, I thought. How long is "soon" to a child? A minute? A month?

Concept books are often shelved separately in the juvenile department of a library, so you can find them easily.

## I Can Read

After picture books, which are usually read to small children, the child is promoted to proudly figuring out, haltingly at first, the letters and words on a page. The popular Dr. Seuss nonsense books come mostly in this category.

Then come simple stories with easy words and short chapters, such as the Frog and Toad stories of Arnold Lobel. Lobel was a genius in a very different way from Maurice Sendak. All his little stories about Frog and Toad are so seemingly artless, so innocent and completely childlike that you will wonder, "Why didn't I write that?" Two small brothers to whom I gave some Frog and Toad books instantly became Frog and Toad. Reader identification! You too may find that the day-to-day doings of little children are more your métier than magic.

After such simple stories come the chapter-books, some of which a fortunate child has already heard read aloud. We have mentioned several such stories.

Reading ability varies greatly at this age. I once gave a niece, age seven, *The Little House in the Big Woods* by Laura Ingalls Wilder for Christmas and thought she would have reading matter for the foreseeable future. She had finished the book before Christmas Day was over. Another child, better in arithmetic than reading, might have taken weeks.

## Starting Your Story

I've given you a wide variety of story types to adopt as your own. Now let's examine the structure of a picture book.

In starting, it is important to plunge right in without preliminaries. You cannot afford the wordage to build up a setting, nor should you need to explain a setting unless it is inextricably involved with the story you have to tell. If you lay your story in some far-off location or adopt an alien child or unfamiliar animal as your character, some things may need to be explained before your story can get under way. This can slow the action. You will need to experiment with words that minimize explanation, and to describe the setting after you have started the action.

The time-honored opening is "Once upon a time." You will not use those words in a modern story because they imply that your story happened long ago. You can come close to this beginning, however.

I make no apology for using examples from my own work because I have written so many books that illustrate the techniques I am advocating.

> *Andy and Mr. Cunningham* begins: "Andy was a boy. One day, coming home from kindergarten, Andy decided he would not be a boy named Andy. He would be a gentleman called Mr. Cunningham."
>
> *The Cat That Joined the Club*: "There was this cat, called Casey, who liked to go where he liked to go and come home when he pleased."
>
> And *The Outside Cat*: "Samuel was an outside cat. He was an outside cat because he never was allowed inside."
>
> *Rockets Don't Go to Chicago, Andy* begins: "One day Andy's mother said, 'You and Daddy and I are going to Chicago to visit Aunt Alice.' 'Can we go by rocket ship?' said Andy. Mother explains rockets don't go to Chicago. Won't it be fun to ride on a train! "I like rocket ships better," says Andy and crawls under the table into his space capsule. The reader suspects right away that somehow trains and rocket ships will merge. Time of day and season do not matter here, and the action is clearly at home.

These simple beginnings are in keeping with the straightforward quality of a picture book. If the nature of the ensuing story is not made clear in your opening statement, as it is in these examples, it should become evident in the next few pages. There are a few words to a page in a picture book because the type is large, so you will still be close to the start of the book when you reach page three or four.

Here is another hint for your story's beginning. Let the first words be a bit of specific dialogue instead of an expository statement. If I had started *The Puppy Who Wanted a Boy* "Once there was a little puppy who wished he belonged to a boy . . ." I'll wager my readers couldn't have cared less. I began, "One day Petey, who was a puppy, said to his mother, who was a dog, 'I'd like a boy for Christmas.' " And I had a book that is still going strong after more than forty years. Later I'll tell you more about the fascinating history of this book.

In a picture book you will not need a lot of background information about your chief character, as you do for older books. All you need is one dominant trait. My *Andy Wouldn't Talk* begins: "Andy was a boy who was too shy to talk to grown-up people." *Gus Was a Friendly Ghost* starts: "There was a friendly ghost by the name of Gus." All the reader needs to know is that Andy is shy and Gus is a friendly ghost.

If you are writing a picture book about an animal, give special attention to names. In *Quiet On Account of Dinosaur* my dinosaur was originally nameless. He sprang to life when I called him Dandy. A name for the teacher, Miss Tutt, and one for the scientist, Dr. St. George, also brightened the story. Offbeat names for grown-ups in a picture book add fun—Mrs. Periwinkle, Mrs. Bucklestone, Mr. Frizzle. You may pick these out of the blue for no reason, just whimsy.

Whether minor characters in a fanciful animal story should have names, sometimes yes, sometimes no. If a dog, a cat, and a mouse live together and may be on something resembling friendly terms, they deserve names. E. B. White assigned his barnyard neighbors delightful names that give them distinct personalities and endear the creatures to us.

If an animal appears just as a species and plays no part in the plot it should be nameless. Don't give a name or a personality to a mouse or a chipmunk that comes to a bad end. Children don't want their friends gobbled up, and if you give a character a name it becomes important.

## The Middle and the End

Your hero, child or animal, will have adventures, and those adventures must work up to an ending satisfactory to the reader. The list of humorous situations given earlier in this chapter offers suggestions for picture-book plots.

Make sure the ending comes fast. Build right up to it and stop. Give your ending a turn that rounds the circle and ties in with the beginning.

The book about Andy, who has decided to be Mr. Cunningham, ends: "Then he ate all the great big banana, feeling just fine, because everything was arranged. And he was still a gentleman called Mr. Cunningham."

As to this cat called Casey, Casey joined a club that served lobster and didn't go home until the club closed in the fall. Joyfully welcomed, he sat on laps for a few minutes. The story ends: "Then Casey went happily off through the dark snowy woods, to join another club if he could find one."

And Samuel, who had been an outside cat, gets his wish: "It's a smart outside cat who gets to be an inside cat!" he said to himself. Then he curled up in front of the lovely fire, and purred.

*Make Way for Ducklings* ends quickly after the Mallards' perilous march, wasting no words to show the ducklings gobbling peanuts and cozily dozing on their island.

*Where the Wild Things Are,* having started with to-bed-with-no-supper, shows Max home again with supper waiting still hot.

## Rhythm

Picture books call for rhythm and repetition. Children like to have words and phrases repeated because they soon know they are coming and feel mighty pleased about knowing. Maurice Sendak uses mostly words of one or two syllables but he repeats "terrible" over and over again. Not only does the repetition lend cadence, but "terrible" is one word that will be added to the reader's vocabulary.

There is a way to help you smooth out the rhythm. A picture book is often printed in a form known as phrase-break, much like a poem. This is easier for children to read. You may write your story in paragraphs and let an editor change it to phrase-break, but if you change it yourself you will detect roughness and unneeded words. You may put the story back into paragraph form if you wish when you have smoothed it out, but you may not want to. *Owl Moon* is written in phrase-break, and the lines read like poetry.

## A Challenge

Picture books are so spare that every bone shows. You can get away with some imperfections in a long book because they may be buried, but you cannot in a picture book. The quality of crispness, of making every sentence move the story along, is important. Look out for useless little words. See how many wells, ands, buts, thens, nows, verys you can take out. You will never miss them but you will sharpen your style.

Study *Where the Wild Things Are* as a superb example of word economy. The entire nighttime adventure evolves from two words Max's mother says to him and four words he says to her, and the exciting story is told in about three hundred and fifty words. Yet even within that concise space the author belies the advice I have just given you and begins almost every page with "and," the word "and" carrying the flow of the story. Actually, I like "and" myself; and often I put down a "but," then cross it out as unneeded. I'll modify my advice and tell you to study your writing and decide whether your style is clipped and concise or free-flowing and poetic, and which is more suited to your story. That should determine to what extent you use those little words.

## The Pictures

In a picture book the pictures are, obviously, important. They will take up half or more of the space. Don't submit suggestions for illustrations to go with your story. The artist will have his own ideas and also understands the use of color in book production and the placing of illustrations, which you do not. The cost of artwork, which may affect the decision whether to use black and white or color, and how many colors, will be considered. The artist and someone in the art department will plan the layout of your book.

You may or may not have any choice as to artist, or opportunity to discuss your wishes. You may never meet the artist. You may ask to see preliminary sketches of the art work for your book, or sketches may be sent without your asking, depending on the editor. You may see nothing at all until the finished book is in your hands.

Here is a reminder of something often overlooked. Author and artist are partners, with joint responsibility for carrying the story. Sometimes a bit of action would be funnier in a picture than it would be in words. Or you would like to delete a sentence in the interest of word economy. Get the message to your artist by way of the editor: "Important! Be sure to show this in a picture."

## A Book or a Short Story?

What is the difference between a picture book and a story in a juvenile magazine? The length is about the same. Picture books are often magazine stories first, but many magazine stories can never be picture books because they do not have a strong plot or pictorial possibilities. Writing for magazines is excellent practice, and it gets your work into print. Just be sure to retain all but first serial rights, because you may have a request later to use your story in a school reader, an anthology, or even as a book. More about this in another chapter.

At the start I told you there are no norms in juvenile literature today. This is especially true of picture books. A story may be fantasy or a realistic story of today. It may be a retelling of an old tale, such as *City Mouse, Country Mouse,* with pictures by Marian Parry, or a legend, such as *The Boy Who Held Back the Sea* by Thomas Locker and Lenny Hort. You may write about some historical character, such as Jean Fritz's Paul Revere or Jack Keats's John Henry. *Sweet Betsy from Pike,* a character most of us know only in song, has been adapted and illustrated by Roz Abisch and Boche Kaplan. You may write in plain narrative prose, poetic lines, true poetry or mere verse, even in cartoon style as Nancy Dingman Watson did in *The Country Goat.* Your book may tell no story at all. There is plenty of scope for your imagination, style, and writing pleasure.

One important element of a book for children that I have barely mentioned is the setting. Your story, for whatever age group, should take place against a background the reader can clearly picture, believe in, and enjoy. The more real you make your background, the better the book will be. We'll go on now to discuss the setting for your story.

# 7

# *The Setting for Your Story*

Once I came home from Europe, visions of old Lisbon, Greek islands, and the high, winding road along the Dalmatian coast embedded in my eyeballs. I ached to share those beauties with my readers.

I could not write just a travelogue; there had to be a story. I decided to send a girl and her parents off to those countries as tourists. I had to have a plot, so I invented a mystery and imposed it upon my settings.

The book was published, but, looking back, I wonder why. The story, though exciting in spots, was contrived, thin, and quite implausible. My editor must have thought my descriptions of those colorful tourist spots were enough.

Later I learned that I was not alone in my determination to adopt a favorite setting first and then devise a story to go with it. Invariably, as I have read those books by other authors, the purpose is obvious, the setting more interesting than the story.

When a setting is foremost in a juvenile book it is usually in a tale with an exotic background, because a thrilling or beautiful place stirs an author into wanting to share the faraway sights with children who may never have an opportunity to go there. The resulting book may rouse in some readers a lifelong yen to visit those sites. If a girl or a boy reading the book is never to venture so far from home, at least you have provided a feast of imagined delights.

But as a fictional story it doesn't work. The book will be

superficial because the author's experience was from outside looking in, a tourist's view.

I went to Corfu because of books by adult authors, Mary Stewart and Gerald Durrell, and to Scotland lured by John Buchan's intrepid heroes in the Highlands. But the only book I read as a child that made me long to go someplace was *Heidi.* I yearned for many years, until I finally got there, to see the Alps, the high meadows where the goats grazed, the Alpine flowers. That book was not written by a tourist visiting the Alps. Mrs. Spyri was born there.

One book that might make a child say, "Can we go there some time?" is Mollie Hunter's *The Wicked One,* laid in the Scottish Highlands with a background of otherworld characters. Mrs. Hunter lives in Scotland and the book grew out of native folklore.

Closer to home, *Where the Red Fern Grows* by Wilson Rawls, with its gentle vistas and sycamore trees, might well make a child long to visit the Ozarks, where Mr. Rawls grew up.

But it is difficult to start with a setting you do not know well and make a book succeed as a story. The background should not stand out apart from the story you have to tell. An effective book is one in which characters drift into the background, which wraps them round like a cloak.

Consider that book beloved by children of several generations, *The Little House in the Big Woods.* What goes on in the little house is completely involved with the big woods around it, and the conflict is not little Laura's but her parents, as they cope with their wilderness environment to feed and clothe and protect their family. Child readers are fascinated by all the details of turning a slaughtered pig into hams, hocks, bacon, spareribs, headcheese, and lard. They wish they could romp with Laura in the fragrant attic where braided onions hang and there are huge pumpkins for play. All this is part of the setting, woven into the action.

But what young readers love most about this book, I believe, is the symbol of the little house as a snug place of complete security in the midst of a dangerous outside world.

This is a setting that is one with story and comes largely from the author's memory.

Another book about a pioneer family is *Sarah, Plain, and Tall,* by Patricia Maclachlan. Sarah, responding to an invitation to become a wife in a family that needs a wife and a mother, comes bringing beauty, laughter, and the colors of the sea she has left behind. The setting presents the essence of Sarah at once. "She came through green grass fields that bloomed with Indian paintbrush, red and orange, and blue-eyed grass." There are more wild flowers, that Sarah and the children pick, and a meadowlark sings. With almost no further words to describe the background, Sarah can be only the Sarah she is. The barn setting presents another side as, laughing, she teaches the children and their father to slide down a haystack dune.

Again, the conflict is not the children's; it is Sarah's. The suspense, though, is the children's. Will oh will she stay to marry Papa, or will she go back to the sea she loves? Sarah grows slowly into this setting and tells them at last that yes, she misses the sea, but she would miss them more. Setting has all to do with the story, but the reader may never notice.

*Sounder* by William H. Armstrong is laid in a black sharecropper's cottage. This is the story of a boy and a coon dog. The sharecroppers' cabins are placed far apart, so the setting is solitary and stark. This family is much poorer than Laura's; sometimes they have no food or scraps for Sounder. The boy goes outside to hear the cold winter wind rising, and the fields are full of dead stalks. Small details, but enough. It is the seeming haplessness of this setting that makes the action remarkable: the boy coming on a white-haired old black man who wants to teach him to read; the boy walking miles back and forth, to the cabin with books on its shelves, and his Mama telling him, in spite of the help she needs at home, it's the important thing to do. The reader knows the boy will walk out of that setting a man.

A book with superb blend of setting and story is *Julie of the Wolves* by Jean Craighead George. Mrs. George is not an Eskimo girl or a wolf, but she spent a summer studying wolves and the Arctic tundra, so she writes as one who knows wolf life well, and from what she learned of Eskimos she knew what skills and ingenuity a young girl would have to possess to survive alone in the trackless snow stretches.

The story is thrilling in its suspense and in Julie's relationship with the wolf pack, the only others alive in that wilderness, who finally accept her. There are many descriptions of the tundra, but they are all from Julie's viewpoint, and every aspect of that snow world presents an obstacle she must overcome.

The author clearly wanted to show this endless snow setting. But she saw much more in that setting, and she says much more in her book. Julie is forced to make many decisions as she fights cold and hunger on her long trek, but her final decision comes on the last page. She has conquered the wilderness with Eskimo skills, but now she knows that the day of the Eskimo and the wolf has ended. She must face the world of the future.

A book that seems authentic enough in its settings to have been written out of firsthand knowledge is *Jonathan Down Under* by Patricia Beatty. This is a story of the little-known Australian gold rush in 1851, and details of the background are interwoven with the experience of a man and a boy prospecting for gold. Enormous research was needed, and we shall talk about research later.

*Turn Homeward, Hannalee*, also by Patricia Beatty, used another historical background, a mill town in Georgia during the Civil War. It deals with the mill workers who were making gray cloth for Confederate uniforms, and the total disruption of their lives by the war. If you cannot live in a place or go to where your action takes place, scrupulous research is the only other answer.

Paula Fox spent several months on the Greek island she writes about in *Lily and the Lost Boy*. She was not just a tourist passing through, she lived among the natives and came to know them, so she can present details of local life. Still, the viewpoint of the chief child characters is not a native viewpoint because these are American children put down in a setting that the author wanted to write about. A story about a native child would have had to grow from a deep knowledge and understanding of problems, limitations, or livelihoods rooted in that setting.

A book that does grow authentically out of its setting is *Jacob Have I Loved* by Katherine Paterson. Laid on an island in Chesapeake Bay, its concerns are with the watermen who make their living from crabbing, and a girl who considers herself trapped by this environment but eventually discovers the way out. Life on the island is governed by hours of daylight and the tides. Details are so vivid they could only have come from experience or astute research, and they are observed from an insider's viewpoint, that of the girl, herself a crabber. Phrases are often intriguing and lend local color.

The story the author chose to place in this little-known but teeming background is an ancient one—a gifted and a seemingly ungifted twin. As you read, you have the feeling that the theme of the story came first to the author's mind, and she knew or discovered a background that would give that story an extra dimension and fresh interest.

In *So Far From the Bamboo Grove* the settings are authentic because Yoko remembers vividly all the details of the bombed hospital train and the railroad station in Kyoto where she and her sister and all the other homeless managed to hold home base. She had the skill to reproduce these scenes for her readers. About her brother's long trek through ice and snow and a stark land that offered no food for his starving body, she had to learn later from her brother himself. She found the words to make that journey memorable.

Jean Fritz's memories are happier ones, but as vivid. She remembers Hankow, her childhood home in China, and she reproduces its teeming life in *Homesick*. The muddy Yangtze River, old women praying on its banks to the River God. Women washing clothes, coolies hauling water. Houseboats swarming with people, chickens, pigs. Junks with eyes painting on their prows. The street of the beggars.

Settings can change in a book as the characters pass through them. *Something New Under the Stars* takes its family halfway across this country, and the environment with its fierce heat and soaking rains provides the conflict that makes the story.

## Familiar Settings

Most of my own books begain with a character and a story I wanted to tell, and the settings are ordinary homes, familiar to many of us. But I did start with a setting in *Ginnie Joins In.* There was an old summer cottage I longed to put into a book because I had such nostalgic memories. What was I going to do with that cottage?

I already had a character from other books whom I could use, so I could have her go there for the summer. Then what happens? There has to be a story. There was no lake there, but I am the author and if I want a lake I can have a lake. Ginnie can swim. Can she dive? Suddenly I have it—the story of her learning to dive and what that triumph does for her. But it all started with that little old cottage.

My books laid on Cape Cod, too, came from love of the Cape and that motivating wish of every author, to share what I loved. I had to devise a character. But once I had the character, as well as the setting, the two had to be closely knit together. I made the setting work for me as an integral part of the plot. Libby, a city child, had to face up to snakes in the woodpile and mice in the attic. When she had put those fears to rest, in later books I brought in some thefts that had actually occurred in a road deserted in winter and local characters I had come to know. I could not have written about Cape Cod in winter had I not lived there in winter myself. My viewpoint had become a local viewpoint, not a summer visitor's.

You do not need a strange or exotic setting for a juvenile book. Children love stories they feel at home in, and a familiar setting can bring instant reader identification. The child starting a book in which a whirling snowstorm rages outside the window will settle down with a little thrill of recognition. A reader who does not live in a snow area may long to see just such a fall of snow.

Even a familiar setting you must know well in all its details to make it real to your reader. If the setting is a fictitious house, draw a diagram of your house. Be sure you know how to get from front door to kitchen and the layout of the bedrooms. Know the furnishings, so you will not have a green sofa in one chapter, a red one in the next. You will not need all of this any more than you will need all the information about your characters, but it will enable you to move people around with the assurance that you will not make a slip. The picture must be clear and unchanging in your mind if you are to make it real. The reader must become the storybook child who lives in the house. After a while he may not be sure whether the house is in the book or down the street.

The same is true for streets, gardens, towns. Each should be its own place, with its special landmarks and characteristic features.

It is useful to keep a notebook of interesting settings. You think you will remember, but you may forget some little detail that will lend realism to a scene. Some authors are never without a notebook for any interesting incident or fact that can be jotted down.

Words to describe a setting and give it exact reality arise from your own skill. Be selective. Avoid verbosity. And replace trite words and phrases with vivid images as you revise.

## Picture Book Settings

Let's consider settings for picture books. Picture book authors cannot afford the wordage, within their few hundred words, to describe a setting, so on the artist devolves the responsibility for presenting that setting.

The grotesquery of the creatures in *Where the Wild Things Are* is what children love. If Maurice Sendak had had to rely on another artist, who had not Sendak's fierce images in mind, the book would probably never have happened, or it could have been, in spite of the wonderful text, a second-rate book instead of a work of genius.

The authentic pictures in *Make Way for Ducklings* are the all-important complement to the text. The story could have happened in another place but it happened in Boston, so real Boston and not an imagined city had to be the setting for the ducklings.

When my ghost, Gus, went to Mexico, my artist, Seymour Fleishman, went too—to San Miguel de Allende, which had given me the inspiration for the story. He said he had never seen a Mexican town and he wanted the pictures to be right.

We had an interesting little experience when Seymour did the pictures for *What's a Ghost Going to Do?* This story is about the old Cape house where Gus had his attic apartment, and that in the book has been sold and might be torn down. Gus put thoughts into people's heads and they turned the house into a museum.

When the drawings were shown to me I was startled. I had pictured a simple old house in traditional Cape Cod style, but Seymour had given the book a fancy Victorian mansion. At first I said it wouldn't do at all. Then we thought about it, Seymour and our editor and I, and we decided that a child reader, insensitive to the beauty of a plain little Cape Cod house, might wonder why all the protest against tearing it down. A Victorian mansion the reader might regard as worthy of rescue. Later, to my delight, I found a Victorian house not far away that really had been turned into a museum.

Footnote to this story: Realistically this house should have been the same one pictured in the previous book about Gus. For the purpose of the story Seymour made this house more elaborate. No one has ever complained.

One book almost failed to get past my editor's desk because, she said, how could you picture a cat's mysterious adventures in pitch darkness? Seymour had no trouble at all. He simply read my text, used his imagination, and drew pictures of what he imagined.

A setting is not just something seen. A setting has sound and smell and things going on. I sat in my garden quietly, day after day, before I began to be aware of all the things going on. A mole creeping out of the ground, chipmunks scampering home cheeks bulging with seed from the bird feeders. A squirrel chasing a catbird. Bees sipping nectar, rabbit munching marigolds, chickadees in line for the bird bath. A hummingbird on the coral bells, goldfinch atop the goldenglow. A butterfly unfolding gorgeous wings on the phlox. A spider wove her rain-sparkled web across the late-summer grass. I had had no idea so much was going on.

Then Mr. Turtle waddled into view and sat, as quiet as I, taking it all in. Suddenly I saw half of a story. I needed the other half, someone to put in this setting, to react to it and in some way be affected by it. It took me a while to find her but I finally wrote *Mr. Turtle's Magic Glasses.*

When children remember a book, long after, it is often something in the setting that they remember. Heidi and the Alpine meadows I shall never forget, but to the story, as I look back, I feel indifferent. I read *The Five Little Peppers* over and over. I recall a few details of the story but mainly I thought if I could just live in an old-fashioned kitchen and scrub the kitchen table, like Polly Pepper, I would be completely happy. I eyed our kitchen table but it did not look amenable to scrubbing. Now, whenever I scrub my maple cutting board I think of Polly Pepper.

L. Frank Baum, creator of the Oz books, wrote another fantasy called *The Sea Fairies,* and the glories of the undersea palace of the queen, with its coral walls, floor aglitter with gems, and couch studded with diamonds, rubies, emeralds and pearls, dazzles my eyes to this day. I have no idea how the story turned out.

Hold in your mind, when you create the setting for your book, that a child somewhere, never known to you, may treasure that place in memory forever. The thought may inspire you to special effort, more studied thought of the words you use. Make them words that deserve to live for some boy and girl.

Let's sum it up. Don't consider you have given your book a setting if you describe the background in a paragraph or two and leave it at that. Know your background well and weave its details and relationship to your characters into the fabric of your story. Be sure your setting has every dimension, appeals to all the senses, not the eyes alone. And, always, show your setting from the viewpoint of the character in the book.

Until now we have discussed pure fiction. There is another large area of writing which many juvenile authors find congenial and interesting and which lends itself more to their writing abilities. On now to historical fiction, biography, and nonfiction.

# 8

# *Biography, Historical Fiction, Nonfiction, and Research*

When I decided this book should pay some attention to nonfiction for children I thought, I've never written any nonfiction for children. Then the *Ginnie and Geneva Cookbook* came to mind and a concept book called *Try Your Hand,* which explored in riddle-and-answer form the many meanings of "hand." Such books fall into an enormous category that includes every subject you can think of. They are pure nonfiction.

Juveniles that come close to fiction in their techniques and story quality are biography and historical fiction, for any age group. History is often written for children by presenting a historical character in the setting of the period that character lived in, in a biography so lively that it reads like a story. If you are a history buff or if your interest runs toward this kind of book, you may have a character in mind already, or you can find one whom you think it would be fun to research and write about.

## For Biography—a Certain Angle

Jean Fritz has written many biographies of historical characters, and I asked her how she picks her subjects. She said, "When I write my biographies it is always because something about that character speaks to me. How could such a brave man as Benedict Arnold betray his country? How could such an oddball as Stonewall Jackson become such a popular hero? I do not look at the school curriculum or ask what is needed or what teachers request."

Jean Fritz looks for a certain angle on a character. Her biography of Paul Revere is the story of Paul's busyness. All the early busyness led to the famous ride, and in later life his boundless energies took him from silversmithing to the bells that still ring in New England steeples and the copper dome of Boston's Statehouse. John Hancock lived, and signed his name, with tremendous flourish. Ben Franklin was the man of ideas. Patrick Henry became the voice of the American Revolution.

Mrs. Fritz made an interesting comment: "Peter Gay, the historian, once said that every biography is also part of or at least related to the author's autobiography and I believe this, although I can't always trace the relation. Yet when my father's sister read my book on Christopher Columbus, she looked up in amazement. 'Why, you know, Columbus was just like your father.' And of course I related closely to Pocahontas, for as a child in China I had seen the superior attitude of white people to those of another culture."

A certain angle is often the clue that starts a biography. Alice and Martin Provensen had been fascinated with flight since the days of flying circuses over the outskirts of their midwestern cities, and they wanted to capture the daring of the first days of flying for children who now take flying for granted. As a symbol of that courage they chose to write in *The Glorious Flight* about Louis Blériot, who made the first flight across the English Channel.

Another author who used courage as a theme was Cornelia Meigs. She wrote *Invincible Louisa*. Just as Jo March in *Little Women* was the mainstay of her family, so was Jo's creator, Louisa May Alcott, all her life. Cornelia Meigs believed that Louisa's dauntless spirit, her philosophy of life, and her belief in God shaped her life and should be passed on to young readers.

## History in Story Form

The juvenile historical novel, for whatever age, differs from biography such as *Invincible Louisa.* It may use either fictional characters—creatures of the author's imagination—or real people, and it involves those characters in events that actually transpired. Marguerite Henry in *Misty of Chincoteague* told a true and exciting story of wild horses. The book has all the elements of fiction, and some real children are the characters. Marguerite de Angeli's *Thee, Hannah* is a story of the gentle Quakers and their assistance to escaping slaves with, one may assume, a fictional heroine. Its wealth of charming details of Quaker life makes up for a fragile story. If historical fiction becomes your forte you will have considerable latitude as to characters, story, and setting, as long as your narrative is rooted in historical fact.

## Research

In writing a biography or a historical novel you may employ much the same techniques, follow the same guidelines as for straight fiction. The main difference is the research needed for nonfiction books. Biography and historical fiction must be based on research, and the more thorough the research the more excellent the book.

Consider biography first. Your exploratory research, if you have found a character you would like to write about, is to get a bird's-eye view of your character. You might well start with the *Encyclopaedia Britannica,* a fountainhead of knowledge. You will also look in *Books in Print* to see what someone else has recently written about your hero.

Consult the card catalogue for books locally available, and then talk to the librarian and ask if the other recent books can be found for you. Also lots of older books. Librarians are interested and helpful people and they know what to look for and where to find it. They may suggest sources of information that hadn't occurred to you.

Immerse yourself in all the books you can lay hands on about your chosen character, making copious notes. Some authors use a notebook or a big yellow pad, others jot notes on cards or scraps of paper. It may take a lot of reading and considering before you settle on your special angle. Then pick out from your notes everything that has a bearing on that theme and put aside for the moment all else. A woodcarver told me when I asked about his work, "If you are carving an elephant, you just cut away everything that doesn't look like an elephant." Later you will need all those other notes and probably more to picture for your readers the period you are writing about. You will use vivid, small details that will interest or amuse children.

Recently I was in the home of a writer who was doing a biography. I mentioned research and he pointed to a carton of books. "You won't read all of them?" I asked, incredulous. "Every one!" said his wife. "And another carton is coming."

Your story, if you are writing biography, should distill the significance out of a life. You do not need to tell all of the truth; what you do tell must be the truth so far as you are able to ferret it out.

You will need to create a sense of history by giving your subject a role in events that actually took place, by personalizing history as textbooks cannot do. You will liven your book with action. You will use some exposition to tie scenes of action together and advance the narrative.

One advantage of partly fictionalizing historical figures is that you can invent words to put into their mouths. You can invent scenes as you imagine they might have taken place. Be careful to avoid any unconscious plagiarism; never use the exact words of another author.

Extensive reading may suffice for research about a historical figure. Jean Fritz says that when she has found her character, because of the questions that intrigue her, "I read to figure them out and then share what I think the story is."

## The Interview

You may choose to record a more recent life, even of a living personality, instead of a character far back in history. Edward Jablonski wrote *George Gershwin.* Nathan Aaseng wrote *Pete Rose.* If you do write about someone living or recent enough to have friends or family members extant, interviews should be part of your research.

The most important interview will be with the subject of your book. Some public personalities are approachable; others may prove reluctant to be interviewed. One eminent biographer never was permitted an interview with a woman whose life he planned to write. In such a case you do the best you can, interviewing others and using all available sources of information.

You locate those people starting with any clue you get hold of—*Who's Who,* telephone books, newspaper files, books. Start wherever you can.

The best approach to an interview is to write a note, identifying yourself and explaining your projected book. Say you will call to ask for an appointment at the interviewee's home.

Make a list of questions that have a bearing on the theme of your book, and make your appointment. Should the interviewee prove reluctant to make an appointment, say you are going to write the story anyway and would appreciate help to assure its accuracy.

If that person sitting opposite you during the interview has been questioned before, you may hear a patter that tells you nothing you have not read. Direct your questions to elicit fresh information, a new viewpoint. If the person proves monosyllabic, answering yes or no, try a question that may bring an involuntary startled response. You may tape the interview, asking permission. You do not have to promise you will send whatever you write. Type your notes as soon as possible while everything is fresh in your mind and you remember every detail of what was said.

## *Stories from History*

If you are writing a historical novel, in which the story is more important than the character, more extensive research will be needed. Marguerite Henry told the story of a great Arabian stallion in *King of the Wind,* and she had to know not only the life of the stallion but about the years when he lived. She wrote letters to historians and librarians. She learned something of the Quaker language from a Quaker authority and about Islam from a professor of comparative religion.

For help in researching her book about Misty this same author turned to such sources as the historian of Chincoteague Island, the Coast Guard, the British Merchant Service, and many libraries.

When Marguerite de Angeli wrote *The Door in the Wall,* laid in medieval England, she read English history. A friend sent her copies of old maps, and in a secondhand bookstore she found a volume of records that covered two centuries. There were masses of detail about life in the period she was writing about. Interesting as all this was, she found little that would actually carry forward the action of her story and she discarded most of it. The records did give her a feeling for life in the Middle Ages.

Patricia Beatty's historical novel, *Turn Homeward, Hannalee,* I mentioned in discussing settings. Mrs. Beatty's story came out of a magazine piece she read, about the Roswell mill hands during the Civil War. In the book's "Author's Note" she acknowledges a debt of gratitude to the Roswell Public Library, which sent photocopied materials, the Indianapolis

Public Library, Cobb County Public Library System in Marietta, Georgia, university professors, and a weaving enthusiast who knew about textile mills.

Mrs. Beatty's "Author's Note" in *Jonathan Down Under* thanks many libraries in this country and in Australia, as well as her own physician and ophthalmologist for information about treatments for pneumonia and trachoma in 1851.

## *Researching Your Contemporary Story*

Stories of today may require research. An outstanding example is Katherine Paterson's *Jacob Have I Loved.* When I mentioned this book earlier I said one had the feeling that the theme had come first and later she had discovered a setting and a story. Mrs. Paterson had been fascinated for years by the biblical stories of siblings and family members—Cain and Abel, Jacob and Esau, Joseph the youngest son. The idea kept bubbling away but she had no story to go with her theme.

Then her son received as a Christmas present a copy of *Beautiful Swimmers: Watermen, Crabs, and the Chesapeake Bay* by William Warner. She began reading it and suddenly she had found a setting. Two of the many islands in Chesapeake Bay were inhabited but isolated. Her story, she knew by now, was to be about a twin who felt isolated because the beauty and talent had gone to her sister. Mrs. Paterson invented her own island, named it Rass for no reason, and began going to the library and to the Bay. She put down on cards and scraps of paper any ideas that occurred to her about events that might take place in the story. She created a place so real that she had to have been there—except that Rass never existed.

For my books I have had to research the history of New Jersey, robots, wolves, how to build a fish pool, and a lot about model railroads and real railroads. Before diesel engines became common I needed to know for a picture book what a diesel sounded like compared with a steam locomotive. I didn't know where to go and listen to a diesel, and I felt very silly writing to railroads saying, "What kind of noise does a diesel engine make?" No one could tell me. I've forgotten how I finally established that a diesel said, "Er, er, er, er, er" instead of "Huchuf, huchuf." All this was amusing, but those letters took time.

In my *Cathy Uncovers a Secret* Cathy uses whatever research tools are at hand to solve a mystery concerning the house she lives in. She consults books in the library, scans old issues of the local newspaper on microfilm, and studies old maps and tax records. She reads history and learns about Civil War politics. I was writing a fictional story but about a real house, so I followed much the same route in writing the book.

Most of my research for books I was able to get from libraries or by correspondence, but there were exceptions. When I was writing *Libby Shadows a Lady* I made a trip from Cape Cod to a New York City police precinct in the heat of July to find out how a given situation would be handled. It was fortunate that I went. I had assumed there would be a security guard in Carl Schurz Park because the mayor of New York lives there. There wasn't. I could resort to a call box to summon the police, they said, there was one at the corner of Eighty-fourth Street. I also learned there was a phone in the police car and what the officer driving the cruiser would say to headquarters.

Another research project was the most exciting adventure of my writing life. Also, it solved a real mystery. I don't think the people in Beaufort, South Carolina, ever accepted my solution, if they heard it. I saw it scoffed at in one local review.

I had seen a strange bright light on a remote road on St. Helena's Island. I heard the local explanation—a headless soldier looking for his head with a lantern. Home I went determined to find out what that light was, not only to write a book about it but because, book or no book, I had to know.

I wrote first to the Beaufort librarian. She knew about the light but she had never seen it. She gave me names of two people who had seen it. She wrote, "I think you should know that voodoo is still practiced on St. Helena's Island." I wrote two more letters and a college student called me. He had seen the light often, watched it turn into the woods.

I read everything I could find on strange lights. Mostly they were dim and flickering, this one was electric. I wrote and I wrote, to every conceivable source of information. No one else had seen the light, all I got back was that legend.

After almost a year of frustration someone said, "Why don't you write to J. B. Rhine?" Dr. Rhine was an eminent parapsychologist known for his work on ESP, and his Institute of Parapsychology was in Durham, North Carolina. I hated to bother Dr. Rhine with what I knew was no psychic emanation, but finally I did. I described the light and the attitude of the people. I said I would like to go down there again but didn't know what to do when I got there.

His reply was prompt. If I would come, and stop in Durham, he would send someone with me. The light probably was nothing but they liked to investigate.

I went and a nice man named Ed joined me. We sat on that dark road where I had sat before, and the light blazed out. In ten minutes, with binoculars and stopwatch, Ed had solved the mystery. We were looking at car lights, so far away on a straight road that we seemed to be looking at one stationary light. It went out when the car dipped into a hollow. It either turned off in the hollow or emerged for a second showing. Coming out of a second hollow, at close range now, the light became a car. But so much time had elapsed that it seemed to have no connection with that baffling light far away. The solution, with elaboration, is in *Ginnie and the Mystery Light*. Research may be reading in a quiet library, or it can mean high adventure.

# Autobiography

Was there a period in your childhood or some special happening that you believe would interest other children? If there was, you probably have in your mind a clutter of memories, a few vivid and stark, others hazy.

You could use these memories to write a fictional book. Harry Mazer's novel *The Last Mission* is a story of World War II and a fifteen-year-old who lies about his age to get into the Air Force. It is based on the author's own experience as a bomber, crewman, and prisoner of war.

But you decide to make your book an autobiographical account, written in the first person. So you must select and shape those memories into the structure of a gripping story.

Go back to the guideline questions in Chapter 5. From somewhere in your memories find a dramatic opening for your book. Then begin to arrange your memories in some kind of order.

You are permitted a little latitude in autobiography. The story you tell must be, in the main, a true one, but you may need to weave in a bit of fiction to carry your narrative on, or you may decide that some change of time or place will make a better and stronger tale.

*Homesick* came from Jean Fritz's childhood memories, but she says in the foreword that her memory "came out in lumps." She did the best she could to arrange events in the right order, but she had to lace some things together with small fictional bits.

*So Far From the Bamboo Grove* is a true story that came out of Yoko Watkins's harsh memories of her own journey to safety. There are minimal changes that in no way affect the validity of the story but were necessary in order to hold to the principle of the single viewpoint. Yoko had to do research to make sure all her dates were correct, and her publisher double-checked. You too would need to assure accuracy of dates and facts. Both Yoko's book and Jean

Fritz's, although they are true stories, are classified as fiction because they read like fiction.

The chapters on characters, conflict, and setting in this book apply equally well to autobiography. Your childhood experiences must make a *good story* for the child reader.

## A Vast Variety

Scan the juvenile nonfiction shelves in a public library and you will be staggered by the variety of books for all ages and the countless authors who have written those books. Should you have a fling with juvenile fiction that doesn't work out for you, you might decide you would have more fun and success with nonfiction.

Like any professional writing, nonfiction demands a good command of English and, when you write for children, a clear and simple prose style. You must have the curiosity about a subject, and the willingness, to set out on what may prove to be a long and complicated trail of research. Whatever your nonfiction subject may be, your facts must be authentic.

There are books about crustaceans, reptiles, how to crack codes, table manners, running a school newspaper, Vikings, the Pyramids. The sounds birds make, cave men, dinosaurs, all forms of nature, animals wild and tame. Babies, the human body.

Some were written by authorities in the field. Helen Roney Settler writes about dinosaurs, and she has made trips to dinosaur excavations, interviewed paleontologists, and read extensively in recent papers about theories and discoveries. Phyllis S. Busch, who wrote *Cactus in the Desert,* has taught biology and general science. Robert McClung, writing about four-footed creatures, moths, butterflies, and bees, was a curator at the New York Zoological Garden.

One remarkable example of research was for the illustrations for *Ashanti to Zulu: African Traditions,* which were done by Leo and Diane Dillon. The Dillons needed authentic information on twenty-six African tribes and they were unwilling to compromise with half-knowledge. They began with their own research library, went on to back issues of *The National Geographic.* From there to the New York Public Library, then to some specialized libraries, even that of the United Nations. Their publisher helped, and embassies were called, obscure books unearthed, and African experts tracked down.

You will find on the nonfiction shelves many books about the problems of teenage girls, usually by authors who can speak with authority. I noticed one book about pregnancy by a social worker; one about parents who are divorcing by a psychologist and a teacher who is herself a divorcée.

Other authors of nonfiction books such as these have developed such skill as researchers that they can write well on a variety of subjects. If you are not a specialist in some nonfiction subject that intrigues you, you can make yourself one, for children's books. Before launching any nonfiction writing project find out what has already been published on the subject.

In historical fiction and biography, as in pure fiction, the characters, the conflict, the setting are techniques you can learn and master. There is one factor beyond techniques, that indefinable quality that lifts a book out of the ordinary—your writing style. What qualities form an author's style? Let's consider them in the next chapter.

# 9

# *Your Literary Style*

I wrote a story about a Persian cat and his reaction to a divorce in the family. I know cats react because one cat I know went into a decline when a human baby appeared on the scene. I thought my story had charm and showed an understanding of cats, and also spoke to the problem of divorce, which many children face.

My editor said no, it wasn't my kind of book. It was a sad little story and didn't show my usual humor.

I knew it wasn't my usual little rollicking animal tale, but the story had the kind of humor cat lovers love cats for. This cat did outrageous things and I thought child readers would understand why he was acting in such a fashion, sympathize, but also be amused. But I was frozen into my kind of story.

I'm sure the advice I have given you, to find your own niche, is sound, but sometimes you might like to break out of that niche. This will be your personal dilemma, to be argued out or worked out with your editor. A story you would like to write may have to go into your dead-letter file, perhaps to be resurrected later.

This points up the importance of being sure, as you choose your niche, that this is the particular branch of children's literature you are going to enjoy working in. And the one that meshes best with your writing style.

As a matter of fact your niche will probably adopt you. Don't aim at any particular audience as you write your first book. Your own style will emerge and that style will head you where you belong—where some editor knows you belong.

# Once Again—Humor

Now let's discuss style as the word applies to your manner of writing, and because no aspect of style in juvenile books is more important than humor, I'm going to start there.

If you possess a childlike sense of humor you should be able to write for the very young, either picture books or stories for the eight-to-twelves. But you must understand the difference between the characters in your book trying consciously to act funny and the reader finding the story funny even when, or even because, the people in the book don't see it that way.

Not that children don't enjoy crazy antics. You may certainly include some. But antics are superficial humor.

In explaining humor in young children's books here is a fair comparison: Doting relatives watching little children play and pretend often find their doings very funny even though the children are perfectly serious in what they are pretending. I once heard a small niece in an imaginary telephone conversation, sounding so exactly like her mother's telephone manner that I couldn't keep my face straight. She was unconscious of being funny. A child reading a book is like those grown-ups. The reader is watching the children in the book do things that seem very funny when the book characters don't mean to be funny at all.

Frog and Toad paddle through their little doings straight-faced, and the child reading the book understands perfectly well what beautiful nonsense it all is and loves it.

Max in *Where the Wild Things Are* is stern and strict, in high command of all the wild things. A mighty serious business. The young reader thinks his control of those preposterous creatures and their obeisance is funny and totally satisfying.

In my *Emerald Enjoyed the Moonlight* the cat Emerald leads Mrs. Bucklestone a merry chase as she tries to get him in for the night. She loses her hairpins and a shoe, tears her dress, and gets her feet soaking wet. Certainly not funny to her, or to Emerald, strolling serenely on. But the escapade tickles readers.

There is a funny little bit in *The Amazing Memory of Harvey Bean.* Harvey has deluded each of his divorced parents into believing he is spending the summer with the other. Very seriously he composes two identical letters. In one he says he is fine, his mother is fine. In the other, he is fine, his father is fine.

And take that automobile ride in *Cracker Jackson,* two eleven-year-olds driving. Cracker clutches the wheel in a nightmare of fright, Goat is on the edge of his seat. Nothing funny to them about that drive. The reader is on the edge of his seat too, and when the ride is over he probably says, "Wow!" And laughs.

In *Alice in Wonderland* Alice trips through her adventures, encounters weird creatures, changes size and all the rest, taking everything in stride with a prim demeanor. Readers have loved the nonsense for generations.

For humor in a children's book you must shrink yourself to the stature of the young reader and get a child's eye view of what is funny. As a matter of fact, good humor will be funny to their parents too, so they won't mind reading the book aloud again and again.

This concept of humor may seem so obvious to you that you wonder why I'm making an issue of it. I hope it is obvious to you, but I've often found such understanding lacking in inexperienced writers.

Once I said to a friend who was trying to write a book for children, "But there's no humor in your book." She pointed out some isolated silly antic of her hero. I suggested several ludicrous situations she might derive from her material, but she couldn't see it.

Ludicrous. That's a good word to keep in mind. Let your style of humor include ludicrous situations. A friend of mine lived on the fourteenth floor and had a mouse in the kitchen. How lovely and ludicrous. How in the world did a mouse get up there? I invented some mouse adventures and wrote *The Mouse on the Fourteenth Floor*.

Once when I went to a funeral a pretty teenager was sorry Grandma had died but her greater interest was in modeling for me the hat she had been allowed to buy for the funeral rites—a smart little black affair with a veil. There is nothing wrong with a little quiet amusement even in times of sadness, and so it can be in a book.

With this understated and straight-faced humor, plus other important qualities, you can write for children of any age.

## Wonderful Words

What are those other qualities beyond the learnable techniques of conflict, characterization, and setting? I am talking about words, wonderful words!

Words are the stuff you the author use to construct your book. If you are a born author you love words. You handle them tenderly, not even aware that the way you use them determines your literary style. But your style, your manner of writing, belongs exclusively to you and is your stock in trade.

The art of language can't be taught as other writing techniques can be, but you can certainly work to improve your skill with words.

Editors get many a manuscript that is basically a good story but told in a poor, prosaic style. This is something the editor usually can't patch up because, even if she had the time, she might be imposing a style that was not very good either.

There are some rare exceptions. Thomas Wolfe was a genius, but his works might never have been given to the world if he had not happened on a great editor, Maxwell Perkins, who devoted his life to making Wolfe's books publishable. There are probably no editors like Perkins now.

Horatio Alger was a prolific writer in the 1870s about street boys who went from rags to riches. His style has been described as a "Matterhorn of clichés," but he was a born storyteller and his books sold more than thirty million copies.

If you turn out to be a story-telling genius like Horatio you may be able to forget about style, also about realistic characters and dialogue. A publisher for that kind of book may be easier to find than one who still maintains high literary standards. One editor said to me, "Unless it's Star Wars or Garfield or Care Bears it's not for us."

But there are first-rate publishers and there are creative editors. If you can add to the all-important good story not only strong characterization, natural dialogue, and humor but also a distinctive literary style of your own, you can produce a first-rate juvenile book.

## *How Good Is Your English?*

We assume your story will be written in correct English. An invaluable guide to good writing, grammar and meaning, and use of words is the little book by William Strunk, Jr, and E. B. White, *The Elements of Style.* You can find it in paperback and it should have a place on your shelf.

I worked with an author who showed a gift for words and had a powerful story, but for whom English was a second language. Her style and her story were her own and her English grammar had to be corrected without destroying the lovely writing. I told her the book should be in the best possible shape before she submitted it to an editor.

Later I asked an editor friend, "Was I wrong? Would they have given the book as loving an editing in the office as I gave it?"

She said, "You were right, and many authors make this mistake. They think if they submit a carelessly written good story someone in the editorial office will fix it up. Editors don't have the time." So be sure you've done all that fixing yourself.

## *Choosing the Words*

Good English is only the beginning. It is easy to be lazy about words. An innocent-seeming sentence may shock you when you dissect it by being colorless or employing some hackneyed expression. The common old phrases come easily from the typewriter keys as you write, but they must be rooted out later. To Harold Ross, one-time editor of *The New Yorker,* every sentence was the enemy, to be attacked, and every sentence should be so to you.

Study your style. Is it what you want it to be—amusing or forceful or sensitive? If not, what is wrong? Try different words, or experiment with the same words in a different order. Why a group of words set down in one order is flat and the same words in a different order are mysterious or stirring, no one can explain, but a dull story may be brought into freshness by skillful rearrangement.

Make strong verbs do the work of adverbs. Instead of having your hero just go into a room, have him march, saunter, trot, hop, run, trudge, jog. Each verb has its own connotation. A verb can be humorous: Make a boy galumph into a room in his boots, a girl flounce out. Instead of having a character say something "in a discouraged tone," make the words she speaks discouraged. "I waited and waited!" There is pathos here.

Put short sentences into brief paragraphs when you want fast action or suspense. For slower effect write long sentences. Use words of Anglo-Saxon origin for a lively style; words from the Latin for ponderous effect.

Words with "l" give a sense of well-being. "K" and "g" sounds are stirring. An "s" can seem sinister and "r" can produce an unpleasant effect. A natural writer doesn't think Now I need an "r" word, the word just comes. Alliteration is a help to smooth writing, and some authors use it unconsciously.

I've said that a picture book, especially, should have the

quality of crispness, but this is true to a great extent of all juveniles. Children like action and brisk onward movement. Scratch out details that have no bearing and slow your story.

## Top Secret

But even choosing the right verb, detecting a trite phrase, and improving word arrangements are not enough. When I discussed single viewpoint I said I was sharing an all-important secret. A ranking secret, in writing juvenile books of literary quality, is making sure you have wrung all possible value—emotional, visual, sensational—from an experience or a scene in your book. Here is where one hundred percent of your concentration must be focussed.

As an example, take two paragraphs from *So Far From the Bamboo Grove,* when Yoko, her mother, and her sister leave the bombed hospital train to continue their journey on foot. In her first draft Yoko wrote something like this: "We passed the burning engine and I saw the tracks stretching ahead." This wording was not graphic enough, did not derive enough emotional impact from this terrible experience of a little girl.

After concentrating, studying, remembering, and revising again and again, Yoko produced this description of her ordeal:

> The burning engines gave tremendous heat as we walked by, their thick iron frames turned red as if to melt at any moment. Through an opening I saw the body of an engineer, burned black. "Don't look," Ko said. Mother kept on walking.
>
> We had been the only healthy ones to get on the train at Nanam, and now we were the only healthy ones to get off. I looked at the long road we were about to take, rails stretching ahead, shining mysteriously in the light of a three-quarter moon.

This is the process that produces superior writing. Study every sentence, every paragraph, for potential development and deepening of their significance, for greater emotional reaction from the reader.

## Those Sensory Impressions

Sensory impressions in your writing can open young eyes and ears to a great deal that there is to experience and enjoy in the world. You can help a child discover beauties never noticed: reflections in a pool, texture of fine fabric, the interplay of sunlight and shadow, smoky smell of autumn leaves. Expand a child's awareness, stir wonder, curiosity or excitement, and you add to the beauty and value of your work. Just don't overload your pages with sensory impressions. Use them sparingly and with a light touch.

You can train yourself for the best possible use of words to convey sensory impressions. Practice isolating one sense and using that sense alone to evoke a mood. The visual sense will be easiest but make yourself look at one thing and see it in its specialty. The color white, for instance, has infinite variations.

Then create a mood by what the ear hears. By what the nose sniffs. Shut your eyes and describe what you feel with your hand—the sleekness of polished wood, roughness of tree bark, caress of cool water—as you want your book character to feel them. You'll sharpen your senses and heighten the sensitivity of your writing.

But don't forget you are writing for children and strange or precious words won't work. Big words, yes. Children love the roll of big words and they help a vocabulary grow. You may use some words that a reader probably doesn't know but are understandable because of the context in which you present them. Never bother with a word list, but keep your language within the ken of the child.

## Your Values

I want to mention one more thing. It's a big thing to bring in casually but it's nothing anyone can teach you: what you have to say to your readers. I don't mean merely the story. And I certainly do not mean a moral. Interviewers are forever asking, "What do you want to say to children? What is your philosophy in writing for children?" I reply hotly, "I am giving them a good story and *that's all*!"

Art is said to be a distillation of the personal values of the artist, the communication of those values. The values come through inevitably as you write. You bring your personality and your interpretation of life to your writing, and these qualities stamp your work with sincerity and individuality.

Never try to convey values by preaching. Do it through the kind of characters you present, the nature of their problems and how they solve them; how they feel about themselves, others, and their lives, and how they act.

It will be the stamp of your personality on your work that sets it off from other writers. And it may be this distinctive quality that will make an editor read further and decide you are a writer worthwhile to encourage and develop and welcome into the fold.

You want to be encouraged and developed. You have some grasp of the various techniques and you hope you have a style. The test is whether you can put it all together in writing a book. Let's see how to go about it.

# 10

# *Weaving the Strands*

I sat facing a blank sheet of paper in a strange typewriter in a friend's home in Seattle. This was to be my third chapter-book. The first two I had accomplished with some boost from an editor. This one I was determined to do by myself, and even on vacation from my job as a copywriter in New York I must waste no time.

But I had never felt so mindless in my life. I had no idea how to start, where I was going in my story or how to get there.

That was before I worked out the idea of a synopsis as a guide. I did stumble somehow through my story. I hope the going will be more straightforward for you.

In the preceding chapters we have treated separately the elements that go into a book for children. You've learned that story ideas are best when they come from somewhere in your own milieu and carry your personal view of life. That the conflict is the story and how that conflict should move along. You understand that you should delineate the people in your book through action and dialogue, but that exposition has its uses. You've read about the special needs of stories for the very young, about fantasy and humor. You understand the meaning of reader identification and the technique of the single viewpoint. You are conscious of the all-important *words* and how they can govern your success.

When you begin the actual writing of a book, you must weave all these strands together in a strong, brightly colored yarn.

We will assume that an idea has developed in your mind into what seems to you a workable book-length story. You have typed out a synopsis, chapter by chapter, that embodies the action.

## You Begin

Finally you are satisfied that you are ready to begin writing your book. You sit down at your typewriter or processor, and you are a little shaky with nervousness and excitement. You must translate the action packed into your synopsis into clearly depicted characters, scenes alive with action and dialogue, conflict that has ups and downs, possesses momentum and carries the reader on and up to a satisfying conclusion. How to begin!

A story must be shaped to the space you have to work with. A young adult book may run to two hundred pages, more or less, with about thirty lines to a page. The middle-age book can be almost as many pages but the type is larger so there will be fewer lines and fewer words to a page. Figure out the wordage and you will know how many double-spaced typed pages you will need and how long your chapters can be. A picture book can be three or four typed pages, a few more, or even less.

Before you begin to type, review in your mind what you have learned about the first page of a children's book. Perhaps reread the first page of *Charlotte's Web,* a book you should own.

You have your detailed synopsis before you. Now, dialogue or setting first? Both? Perhaps you can have two girls talking. You begin to type. You make your heroine say something. No, those words have no connection with the story to come. You ex them out and do it differently. Now what she says gives some small clue to the action about to develop. You have made a beginning.

If your book has begun with dialogue, you have started, properly, with a scene. Now you may need a bit of expository writing to explain your initial situation more fully. Perhaps you need to introduce another character. Then probably you will continue your initial scene with its dialogue.

Brief exposition—the author explaining—can take you to a second scene. Or should the first scene extend through the entire first chapter? You will need to think about it at your typewriter, perhaps pulling out more than one sheet of paper to begin afresh. (Save every discarded sheet. Use the other side for rough drafts.)

But finally the action, dialogue, and exposition will begin to fall into place, a bit clumsily perhaps.

You are moving along in chapter one now. Read over what you have written. Not perfect, by any means, but it will do for a first draft. You must move toward the end of the chapter on a rising note of interest or suspense so the reader has simply got to go on to chapter two.

You pull your first draft of chapter one from the typewriter and read it. Many things about it you don't like. And it is probably too short. That is good, because you'll be filling it out with details and minor action. Don't let it run too long, or an editor may ask you to cut.

## You Move Along

On second reading you see that at least everything essential is there. You have established the identity of your main character. You have indicated the nature of the problem—what the story will be about. The conflict has begun.

As you study your manuscript you think perhaps you should hold this scene a little longer, fully to engage the reader's emotions. Is the next scene too long? Have you made the setting realistic? Can you make that dialogue say more about the people in the book? Is it *interesting?* Does the chapter ending have a real hook?

You see improvements that can be made. You see tired expressions. Your brain and your fingers itch to fix things up. But not yet. Not until you have pounded out all those ten or more chapters. Chapter one is enough for today. You put check marks or notes in the margin to remind you of work to be done.

But now you can see where chapter two should start. Before your next-day session with the typewriter, chapter two with its scenes, connected by exposition that moves the story forward in time, may be fairly clear in your mind. Not always. You may sit at your typewriter and ponder.

If you are writing a picture book, the only difference in the actual writing is that you type the entire story at one sitting. Then you go over it and over it, scribbling in changes and retyping, perhaps many times, before you put the story away for a rest of days or weeks while you go on to other writing or catch up on neglected chores.

## Your Working Time

As you plan your working time, a chapter a day is enough—ten pages or even fewer than that. I am speaking of your first rough version, just the skeleton of a book one step beyond your synopsis. You will write those ten pages over many times—revise, correct, expand, enrich. Ten or so rough pages may not seem like much for a day's work, but unless you are a super-being you will find that those pages take a lot out of you. It is not just the physical typing; you are putting forth a tremendous creative effort.

And you have other duties. You may be a mother with a clutter of everyday chores and concerns or a commercial artist who commutes to an office. Some days may not leave one moment for writing. But the flow of thought and expression should not be interrupted for too long. If you let days go by you will lose some of the momentum.

You will find time if the urge to write is a driving force. Many a successful book has been written on the kitchen table after the children have gone to bed, or scribbled during lunch hour.

Perhaps you will not even glance at chapter three and chapter four as you finish them, although sometimes you will need to look back to make sure one chapter relates as you want it to to the next one.

## Your Subconscious Helps

When you are at this stage of writing a book your mind will do a lot of work while your body goes through alien motions. Your subconscious keeps on while you sew on a button or drive the car, or you wake in the morning and find that something has added itself to your story, or your approach is out of character, or an incident is needed in chapter four or you build up to your climax too fast.

Somewhere along the line, as you write, you may realize you lack some information that you need for accurate or graphic detail. Perhaps you can look it up in a book in the library. Or perhaps you cannot avoid doing some real research to authenticate facts or background.

You will probably do major research before you start your book. It is mostly small details that stop you as you suddenly realize you don't know enough to present them realistically, however casually. Elementary your facts may appear in the book; they must be absolutely correct.

If you are unsure of something as you write the first draft, do it the way you imagine it might be, so your writing will not be delayed. Whatever research is needed by reading, correspondence, phone calls, or travel, do in your nonwriting hours.

Also, in your first draft, don't break the flow of writing by waiting to find some exact word. Put in any expression, with a checkmark in the margin, or leave a blank for the time being.

Now and then in nonwriting moments go back to some of the guidelines, the story you are writing clear in your mind, and see how it seems to be holding up. Are you staying on the track of the main conflict? Have you held to the single viewpoint? If you feel a sudden suspicion about your technique pick up the manuscript and read what you have written so far. If your instinct was right and you find some basic inconsistency in the way you are working out the conflict or a character, go back and change something right now. What happens in chapters one or two will determine all that follows.

So, trying to follow those guidelines and with one eye on your synopsis, you type your way through the ten or more chapters.

This first draft will be rough, but the hardest work is behind you. You have got it down on paper. You have woven those strands of action, character, and setting together, though not yet in perfect balance. Additional action, accuracy of detail, and refinements in wording will come later, when you have rested, your manuscript has rested, and you return to it with fresh perspective.

## You Put It Away

When you finish your first draft of a book, my advice is to put it away for weeks, resisting all temptation to read it. The longer you leave a story before you go back to it, the more clearly you can see its flaws and what to do about them and the less painful it is to strike out some favorite part that you see now the story does not need. It is easy to put a long book aside because the writing has been a chore and you are glad to forget it for a while, but with the picture book it is hard to wait. You are always sure, for the moment, that what you have written is good, and you are avid to get at it again. But put it away you must. In the meantime you can start work on the outline of another book.

## You Revise

When you finally take your story out, first read it through from beginning to end, not correcting. You may find with surprise that it is better than you thought. You had terrible forebodings. Now you take heart. And your mind has been working while you rested from the writing. You are eager to expand and refine and improve.

With a picture book, oddly, your reaction will be different. It seemed perfect just after you had written it. Now you see it needs a lot of rewriting.

Now you must become your own severest critic. You go over the manuscript a second time, more slowly, and add new marginal jottings. Perhaps you can see that the story moves too slowly or a transition is made too quickly, or you have too much expository writing or too much unrelieved dialogue. Going back to all those checkmarks in the margin, you attack one by one the places that need improvement.

This is the time to insert the results of the research you have been doing and to replace your imagined version with the real thing.

You scratch out, scribble, revise until even you cannot read what you have written. Retype and do a repeat performance.

Preliminary scribbling as you first began thinking about your book was probably done in longhand; in my case it was always in a comfortable chair. I am assuming that you typed your synopsis and will type your book. Professional authors usually work on a sophisticated electronic typewriter or a word processor. (But cheer up. I still use a portable, not even electric.) Authors have been known to write an entire book by hand, but it is easier to see flaws in typed copy without too many corrections written in than it is on a handwritten page. Should you be so unwise as to submit handwritten copy to an editor, the chance of its being read might be slim. Some editorial offices do have a rule that every manuscript must be looked at.

Now go through the story, perhaps just in your head, for a different kind of revision. Follow each character through the string of events to make sure you've been consistent throughout. Be certain there is nothing you yourself know so well that you have neglected to explain to your readers. Examine your dialogue. Is it natural? True to the character speaking? Does it always relate to the story?

Finally, study your language closely and replace run-of-the-mill expressions with words that are sharper, more sparkling. Scrutinize every small bit of action for development and greater emotional impact. And check any questionable spelling.

Make a readable copy and again allow some days to go by. When you pick up the manuscript again and give it a reading, which may not be the final one by a long shot, there will still be places to refine. No matter how many times you read it you will find ways to improve the wording. You may do a lot of rearranging, clipping, and pasting. You may type an entire book or parts of it three or four or more times before you are ready to send it out.

## The Title

Often the title, important as it is, comes after you have finished the book. A title may arise naturally from some place in the story, so look for a lively phrase and put it on the title page. Alliterative words in the title are good. A verb is often better than a static noun. The word "little" appeals to small children, and for older readers such words as "spy" and "mystery" are said almost to guarantee sales. They have been used so often, however, that you might seek other words that convey the same excitement.

## Off It Goes

You have finished your book. You have typed it neatly, double-spaced with wide margins, on white paper, on a processor or a clean typewriter with a fresh ribbon. You have a carbon copy or at least one photocopy. Even this final version you have read over and over again for typing errors and possible improvements in the wording. You put your name and address on the first page.

You write a covering note to the editor you have determined you will send your story to. You put your manuscript in a large manila envelope, address it, find out the first-class postage rate at the post office, enclose a return envelope, and hand your packet in.

You come out of the post office into the fresh air, and the weight of the world seems lifted from your shoulders. You have done the best you can. It is up to the editor now.

To many people, and perhaps to you too as an inexperienced author, the role of the editor is ambiguous. Let's look into some very important things that an editor can do for you, and at what happens once you have mailed that manuscript.

# 11

# What Does an Editor Do?

Assembling some income tax figures, I listed a bill for taking an editor to lunch. My accountant looked at me quizzically. "What," he inquired, "does an editor do?" In other words, was that deduction a legitimate expense? I had lunched to keep in touch with an old friend and to ask her some important questions.

Every published book has an editor. The editor is the necessary link between you and the book-buying public, and there is not much point in writing unless your book reaches readers in the juvenile public. You know that, so editorial approval is the light at the end of the tunnel. The light may seem far away. But when you scanned those juvenile books on the library shelves you felt some awe at the hundreds of people who had written books for children and had them published. If they could, tell yourself, I can too! Assuming of course that you are serious about writing.

Every route to the book-buying public, via an editor, is different, so let's set up a hypothetical case, an optimistic one.

A good way to find a likely publisher is to look at books similar to yours in the library and note the publishers. A guide to manuscript markets, also in the library, will give you addresses and usually the names of juvenile editors. If you do not have a name you may call up and ask; using the name is an initial courtesy. And how do you start a letter if you have no idea to whom you are writing? If an editor-in-chief in the juvenile department is named, address your letter to her. I say "her" for convenience. Most juvenile editors but not all are women.

Whether you write a letter before you send your manuscript, to ask if your book has a chance of being considered, depends on the kind of book. Such a preliminary letter is called a query and we'll talk about queries later. For picture books, no query, because even if you offer an appealing idea, how can the editor know what you, an unknown, would do with that idea? Editors are besieged by manuscripts and they must make a judgment as to which ones to let through the gates.

For longer fiction, sometimes a query, sometimes not; consult the publisher's listing in the manuscript guide. But yes, you may query on nonfiction; the subject may interest an editor. If not, you save the time and expense of sending your manuscript.

Query or sans query, you have sent off that manila envelope, and you begin to learn the first hard lesson of a writer's life: You wait, and you wait, and you wait. To fill the time you should be busily occupied with your next book.

Until now you have been in competition with no one but yourself; you have tried to make every piece of writing better. Once your manuscript reaches an editor's desk you are competing with other authors whose stories are also awaiting consideration.

## The Case of the Lucky Author

To return to our happifying hypothetical case, eventually your manuscript is read, in a large publishing office perhaps not by the editor-in-chief to whom you addressed it, but by a subordinate who sifts out hopeless stories. There may be one or more senior editors in that office, plus a managing editor, the next lower rank.

Something about your story catches the reader's eye; it stands out from the usual manuscripts. She reads it again and decides it merits being passed on to the editor-in-chief. If that editor agrees, your story will probably be read by other staff people or an outsider with trusted editorial experience.

Many editors look not for a work of potential genius but for a well-written good story that requires little alteration and that they are confident will make money for the publisher. Some see no reason why they should teach new writers how to write.

Our hypothetical editorial figure is different. She wants a good story but she also values literary quality. She has imagination, and she sees possibilities for a rather special book if she can draw them out. She, or one of her staff, writes you and makes some constructive suggestions about the manuscript, promising nothing. She has no idea what you will do with these suggestions.

## *Your Editor's Role*

Encouragement from an editor warms you no end. You thought your story was right the first time but now you see it through other eyes and you recognize that the criticisms are valid. You do the best you can in revising and send the story back. After another long wait the revised manuscript may come back again. Better, but here are some more thoughts.

Let us assume this process goes on for quite a while. You are beginning to learn there are no miracles; getting a really good book published is hard work. If you live near the city where the editorial offices are located you may in time be asked in for a talk, even be invited to lunch. The editor is curious about this person who, obviously, can write, and she wants to take a look.

Here is where a good editor's value to an author shows itself most strikingly. Across a desk—a luncheon table is better or it may have to be by letter—you toss the weaknesses of a story, which are almost always there, back and forth until a meeting of the minds is reached.

Even for an established author revision may be major. Katherine Paterson knew even when her editor liked *Jacob Have I Loved* that months of intensive rewriting lay ahead. And her editor helped her, she said in her Newbery Award speech, to weave *Bridge to Terabithia* into a real story with a beginning, a middle, and an end.

Finally, in our hypothetical case, your book is actually accepted. The editor has helped you write an acceptable book, a much better book than it started out to be.

Mind, this doesn't happen to everyone, not even almost everyone. But some authors are going to make it and we are assuming in our chronology of events that you'll be one of them.

Now you find that writing the book was only step one, revising under editorial direction step two. Step three begins. The final copy of your manuscript is in, and the editor is satisfied at last. You have word that a contract will be coming, and again you wait and you wait. Finally the contract arrives. We'll discuss contracts and what you should know about yours in the next chapter.

Then comes the long process of production, and the editor sees you through. First your edited manuscript is sent you—your typed copy with a copy editor's marks, questions, and notes. The copy editor is down the line in a large publishing office. In a small publishing house one editor may do everything.

Many of the revisions are of punctuation or spelling; the publisher probably has a style book. If you are new to publishing you may not understand some of the editor's markings. Here are a few of the most common:

| | | | |
|---|---|---|---|
| Comma | ^, | Delete | del |
| Period | ⊙ | Leave as typed | stet or |
| Colon | :/ | or printed, | dots under |
| Semicolon | ;/ | ignore correction | word |
| Apostrophe | ˅' | Small caps, 2 underlines | ═══ |
| Quotes | ˅" ˅" | Caps, 3 underlines | ≡≡≡ |
| Paragraph | ¶ | Italics, 1 underline | ___ |

The editor may indicate how she would like you to make changes of your own on the manuscript.

But some alterations may be changes of wording that you cannot accept. Even as a beginning author you should not let an editor make a revision that alters your style of writing. Be nice about it but be firm. Your style is you and you must keep it that way.

If you have second-thought changes or additions of your own, now is the time to make them. Changes on proofs, which come next, cost money.

Once my editor asked if she could skip the edited manuscript, to save time, and just send me the proofs. When the proofs came I was furious. Some young copy editor, unfamiliar with my style, had so revised my writing that it didn't sound like me. I changed everything back. My editor said the type for the entire book would have to be reset.

Fortunately I lived close enough to my New York publisher to go in to the office. I spent an entire wearying day going over the proofs with my editor. I compromised some and the editor, apologetic, compromised too. We managed to avoid the costly and time-consuming resetting of the type and we never skipped the edited manuscript again.

## *If It's a Picture Book*

If your story is a picture book, artwork must be considered. Beginning writers often ask, "Should I get an artist?" No, the publisher does that, unless you are an artist yourself qualified to illustrate your own book. You would have to understand the technicalities of book illustration.

The publisher's art department has lists of artists, and there are discussions in the office, in which you have no part, as to which one will be right. Which artist is good with child figures? Animals? Machines? A copy of your story is sent, and usually the artist is glad to undertake the assignment unless too much other work is on hand to meet the deadline. Will the pictures be in color or black and white? If in color, how many colors? The artist and the art department get busy making a dummy.

Some editors do not voluntarily show the dummy of a picture book to the author, but you may ask to see it. A dummy is paper folded into sheets, like a book, and shows how the lines of your story will be placed in relation to the artist's preliminary drawings. Seeing the dummy and the rough illustrations can be a big help. There may be points in your story you would like picked up in the pictures, and the artist has missed them. You may see possibilities for more humor in the illustrations.

An editor, if so minded, can be an invaluable liaison between you and your artist. She can create a climate for exchange of ideas. She may have some good ideas herself about the artwork. Her suggestions, passed along to both you and the artist, may spark new thoughts in both of you and improvements in the pictures. This three-way collaboration can result in sharper, funnier, more apt pictures and a much more charming book.

On the other hand, you the author may have little part in the production of your picture book. You will be told what artist has been selected but you may never meet him or her. You may be shown samples of the artist's work, or you may ask to see some samples. As a beginning author you will not be too demanding. Later, as you gain confidence, you may speak up if you don't like the samples. I was shown advance sketches of artwork for *The Ginnie and Geneva Cookbook* because I had stipulated that the pictures of kitchen utensils must be so realistic a child could not fail to recognize an egg beater or ring mold or strainer in the kitchen. These drawings were not, and my publisher found another artist.

Once when the artwork was shown me I saw a train on the wrong track. Another time I had seen nothing of the artwork during production and I so disliked the pictures in the finished book that I asked to have the book taken off the market, but it was too late.

## Title—Dedication

Your working title for the book may be acceptable to the editor; if not, she can help. She has experience. She may even consult the sales department about the kinds of titles that help sell books.

If you would like your book dedicated to someone, make this request early, because a spot must be found. This will not always be a separate page, as you would like. It may be on the copyright page.

## Promoting Your Book

After your approval of the proofs comes the longest wait, because the production process may take as long as a year, but now there is no dreadful suspense, because you know your book is real. And you are working on your next book with wisdom gained from the first one. Finally you receive your advance copy.

Now begins step four: The publisher's public relations and advertising departments get busy promoting the sale of your book. Your contact will still be your editor. You may be asked to give talks here and there, to autograph books at a bookshop or to go on a speaking tour. On any tour you are asked to take your publisher will plan the trip, make your plane and hotel reservations, and foot the bill.

# The Case of the Unlucky Author

The scenario of what happens after you send the manila envelope may be very different. In most cases a book is rejected on the first try, sometimes again and again after many tries. It may not be a bad book, but perhaps the publisher has recently put out a similar book. Or your book is not in line with this publisher's needs. The editor may think it's a good book but wouldn't make enough money. It may require too much editing.

Your book may be rejected after the editor has given you initial encouragement because you cannot or will not make the changes suggested. If after a couple of efforts at revision the editor still says no, write that one off.

This rejection is a bitter disappointment but one you come to live with. At first you may refuse to accept the reasons for rejection. You compose sarcastic letters to the editor, which you never send because after you have slept on it, or not slept, and have calmed down and had the heart to look at your story again, you decide reluctantly that the editor is right. Now you see things you have done badly.

And, before long, the flickering flame of creation revives. You take a hard, honest look at your work. You have learned from the editor's comments. You get to work again. Your next version or your next book will be better. You are becoming a professional author, ready to take the disappointments and criticism that are bound to come along with your successes.

If the initial rejection leaves no door open you may send your story right off to another publisher. Many highly successful books were rejected dozens of times before they found a publisher. One author told me her book had made the rounds of all possible publishers twice before it was accepted. An editor must reflect the policies and needs of the publisher, and it may take a number of tries before the needs of a publisher and your story mesh.

Occasionally a letter may say the editor would like to see something else. See that she does, and soon. If she rejects several manuscripts it should dawn on you that she listens to a different drummer. Don't waste any more time with that publisher.

All this is the normal course of events with a new author, even with authors who finally achieve success. The secret is sticking to it.

## Your Editor and You

Editors of children's books reach the post of editor-in-chief by a number of roads. This has been called the accidental profession: few have risen because of academic training in editorship. Some come up the ladder from other departments such as sales promotion; they have learned the field through wide contacts in the publishing industry. Others gain experience in a minor editorial position, prove their expertise, and either move up in the same publishing company or win promotion by going to a different publisher. Some editors have been children's librarians or gained experience in bookshops. Experience is the keynote, and often a record for picking successful books.

If you sell your first book to an editor whom you like and come to trust, try to stay with her. Some authors seem always on the move from one publisher to another, sometimes because they have to, to sell their books, but sometimes in search of a higher royalty or better fringe benefits.

A good editor, if you stay with the same one through a number of books, is like the primary nurse in a hospital. She is the one you turn to not only for advice about your writing but for complaints or requests you wish to make. She can become a friend and guide. You will trust her as a person and a professional authority, and if she moves to another publishing house or retires or dies, you feel like a ship without a rudder.

If your editor does move to another publisher you may send your next book to her instead of to the original publisher, unless your contract gives the first publisher the right of first refusal of your next book. The rights to the book you have sold to a publisher remain with that publisher, not with an editor who moves somewhere else.

## *A Changing Industry*

Editors move around a lot these days because of tremendous flux in the publishing industry. Many publishing houses have merged with others or have been acquired by some huge conglomerate. Editors are affected because a department may be eliminated or merged with another that already has an editor. Many editors are more interested in being corporate officers, with eye on the dollar, than they are in the traditional role of the editor as a maker of authors. Publishing is big business, and juvenile books are a large piece of the publishing industry.

## *An Editor Can Be Your Friend*

I have said that an editor may become a personal friend; this is a relationship to be treasured. Magazine editors too can become friends. We'll talk about sales to magazines later. One editor of a magazine to whom I sold several serials always wrote me when she planned a trip to New York, and we had dinner. We not only liked one another, but talking over her editorial needs was helpful. The editor of a juvenile magazine and I lunched often. I learned his likes and dislikes—especially his dislikes—and this was a helpful guide as to whether to send him a story. Other editors, whom I never met, showed themselves through our correspondence to be cordial individuals.

## *Some Negatives*

A good relationship must survive some negative reactions and rejections. There will be times when you and your editor disagree and cannot reconcile your differences.

I wrote one book that my editor did not like at all. We argued, over a luncheon table. Finally she said, "Catherine, do you want us to publish this book? We will if you want us to." Instantly I backed off. In my heart I trusted her judgment more than I trusted my own. I knew what I wanted to write, but she knew what librarians and schools would buy. Why take a chance on a book the editor thought would be a flop?

And on one dreadful day in my life my editor rejected two books. I had written them during a difficult period when someone was dying, and my mind was too tired to do a good job. I discarded both of those stories but I kept the idea of one and wrote an entirely new book.

Some editors wish to keep the author-editor relationship strictly business. This will be evident in their letters, courteous but brusque. This you must respect. Every editor is different; editors are people. One can be a fine editor and remain impersonal.

One hears of editors who give no help, who seem indifferent and fail to answer letters. I cannot help wondering whether sometimes the author may be partly at fault; whether the image he or she projects in correspondence turns the editor off. An overly personal approach, sarcasm, a smart-alec attitude, or too eager emphasis on money-making could do that.

The opposite may be true. An editor may turn you off in the first letter or by the kind of stories she says would be acceptable. Write off that editor, that publishing house.

Sometimes when an editor rejects a story without constructive suggestions it is because she simply does not know how to help you. Not all editors are creative people. Some can spot the weak points in a story but they can't tell you how to correct them. Just having those weak spots pointed out can be a help. You suddenly see them for yourself and you get out of the trap by going back to the guidelines and studying your story anew.

The experience of award-winning authors, however, usually reflects a close working relationship between author and editor. If you start out as an Unlucky Author, and almost everyone does, never, never give up until you are a Lucky Author with an editor!

If your manuscript is sold by a literary agent—and there will be more about agents in the next chapter—the sequence of events I have outlined will not take place. Your book may be accepted before an editor has read the entire manuscript because someone has decided, after reading a couple of chapters, that it will make money. You will still have an editor, who will correct your grammar and punctuation, question your facts, suggest improvements, and help in many ways, but this editor may be almost an unknown figure, at least at first. Your relationship will be on a less personal level and you may have a different editor—and a different publisher for your next book.

Now let's see what you need to know about agents and other aspects of the business of selling a book.

# 12

# *The Business of Writing*

Recently I met someone who was so naive as to inquire, "How much does it cost to get a book published?" The query floored me; it seemed inconceivable that anyone could entertain such a misconception about publishing.

There really are publishers who are paid to publish a book; they are called vanity presses. A vanity press is for someone who has tried in vain to sell a book to a legitimate publisher and is so anxious to get it into print that he will pay what it costs. A vanity press may be used to publish something of personal value, such as a family history. But your manuscript is a product which you hope to get published and be paid for.

The question of that novice made me realize that all newcomers to publishing have questions about matters that seem common knowledge to experienced authors. I had wanted to limit the scope of this book to writing; business details of my profession have caused me impatience and annoyance. But I have been forced many times to pay attention to business and I decided my book would be of greater value to new writers if it answered some questions that are often asked.

Store this information away, then go back to your writing. Never let a preoccupation with the business end take time, energy, and thought away from your writing.

You want to know what chance you really have of getting

a book published. And, when you do sell a book, what you should watch for in the course of the sale and later. Let's get to your questions and some answers.

## What Chance Do You Really Have?

It seems a paradox when more and more publishers are merging with others, but publishers' profits on hardcover juvenile books have tripled over the past decade; sales of paperbacks have almost quadrupled. Bookshops selling just children's books have sprung up throughout the country. A fresh market for any juvenile book opens each year as children advance in their reading ability and interest and another group follows right behind.

High sales encompass all kinds of children's books and expand the opportunities for authors. Yet a good editor will tell you that there is a dearth of top-quality juveniles. This is where your expertise in writing can count.

## Should You Find a Literary Agent?

A literary agent is a go-between who handles the business of selling a book for you. You will find agents listed in a good market guide.

Traditionally, most agents have not handled books for children. But juvenile publishing has experienced an unprecedented boom, and children's books are generating much larger profits than in the past. Publishers are giving special attention to their profitable juvenile divisions, and more agents are taking on children's books. Sophisticated procedures common in selling adult books are penetrating the juvenile field.

I have suggested the individual approach to editors because the author-editor relationship is precious and may be diminished if you work through an agent. Also, it may not be easy to find an agent who is willing to take on an unknown author, unless your work shows exceptional character.

But that valuable working relationship between author and editor no longer exists in some publishing houses, partly because editors move around so much, and if after several attempts to reach an editor you are getting nowhere, you might consider seeking out an agent.

There are advantages to having a literary agent. Once you become a known author you may decide that business details are onerous; you want to put your energies into writing books, not selling them. A good agent is familiar with the market, knows editors personally, and can shoot your story to a likely target more quickly than you could yourself. An agent may be able to negotiate a higher advance than you could, and your contracts will receive the scrutiny of a practiced eye.

Your agent will collect probably fifteen percent of your royalties and any subsidiary rights income as his/her fee for as long as your book stays in print.

If you are fortunate enough to establish a good editor relationship with your first book, you will have a receptive market for other books and you probably do not need an agent.

## How Do You Find a Publisher?

I suggested earlier that you go to the library, find books similar to your own, and make a note of the publishers. If a publisher especially appeals, you might write and ask for a copy of its catalogue to see what books have been published recently.

Also in the library, consult a guide to manuscript markets. The most complete is the *Literary Marketplace,* which calls itself the *Directory of American Book Publishing.*

The contents include names of United States book publishers, grouped by geography and subject matter. The names of juvenile editors are given. The directory also lists junior book clubs, awards, organizations, agents. This is a huge tome.

If you have decided on a publisher to whom to send your story you will find that publisher easily in the directory. If you are in a quandary about where to send the manuscript, consult the list of publishers who put out juvenile books, then check the listing of each.

A publisher's listing will tell you what type of stories that house is interested in seeing; whether a manuscript must come from an agent; whether an unsolicited manuscript (one that has not been asked for) will be read; whether to send a query. It will tell you whether the publisher pays a royalty; all first-class houses do. It may offer to send guidelines for submissions.

Check to see when a publishing house was founded. A new or relatively recent publisher is a better bet for you. It is building up its list of authors and will extend a warmer reception than the old ones that already have many authors they can count on for profits. This research will narrow your list and save wasted effort.

The mysterious letters SASE in a listing mean "Self-addressed stamped envelope." This is a must when you send a story—an envelope with enough postage to bring your manuscript home if it's not welcome. You may find the term "Imprint" in a listing. This means a line of children's books within that publishing house handled by an editor who has earned the the honor of having "her own imprint." These might be termed Bluebird Books, Sparrow Books, or whatever.

## How Do You Query an Editor?

A query is a letter to a juvenile editor asking whether the book you have written or hope to write might at least be considered. The publisher's listing usually tells whether to query and on what type of book. Nonfiction usually calls for a query. The listing may indicate what you should include: usually a synopsis of the book and a couple of sample chapters. Send a covering letter telling something about yourself and your background, why you are qualified to write this book, and why the book is important. Perhaps you can say, having researched it, that no comparable book is on the market. Mark the envelope "Query" and enclose an SASE.

## What Is Multiple Submission?

A multiple submission is sending a manuscript simultaneously to more than one editor. The practice is common in the adult field as a timesaving measure and sometimes to initiate competition for a book.

Multiple submissions are being used more and more in the juvenile field, but a few houses have a specific policy of not considering them. A listing in a literary guide may tell you a publisher's policy in this particular.

An editor told me, "There's really no general information one can give writers about the best submission procedure because each house has its own preferences. A writer really has to develop his/her own check list. I tell aspiring writers that the only *must* is to state in a cover letter if they are making a multiple submission. Otherwise, they can follow their inclination (as long as they don't have information about the publisher's policy to the contrary).

"In my opinion," this editor concluded, "an unpublished writer is probably better off not complicating a submission."

You may certainly query more than one editor, hoping you will receive at least one invitation to send in your story.

## Should You Get an Artist?

The publisher will choose an artist unless you are found qualified to illustrate your own book. If you are an artist, or if you are collaborating with an artist, send with your story copies —not originals—of drawings that the publisher may keep.

## What Should You Know About Your Contract?

All right, you have found a publisher. You have sold your book. The next item of business is the contract.

A contract is an agreement between you and your publisher. It stipulates certain things that you the author agree to do and other things that the publisher agrees to do. You are going to sign this contract, which means you accept its provisions, so read your first contract carefully. The contract is written in legal language, and if legal language and documents cause surges in the stomach you will have to force yourself, but read it. Once you have grasped the intent of each of the many clauses, you will never need to study another contract so closely. Some are simpler than others, but their basic provisions are the same. If your second contract is with the same publisher just compare the two quickly.

The contract will state that you are the sole author of the work, that it contains nothing libelous, and that you grant to the publisher the right to publish it within certain geographical areas. You assign to the publisher the right to license other publishers for different editions and certain subsidiary rights.

The publisher agrees to publish your work at its own expense within a stated time period, to register copyright, to pay you at a given royalty rate with an advance payment. The publisher agrees to give you ten copies of the book, five if this is a picture book, and to sell you more copies at a forty percent discount.

These are the principal provisions, but read the entire document and if a clause is unclear ask your editor to explain. The Authors Guild advises authors of juvenile books to watch for so-called "nasty" contract clauses. The Guild says even literary agents may overlook smaller points that are disadvantageous to authors.

The Society of Children's Book Writers has a pamphlet, *A Guide to Contracts,* which will be sent you for twenty-five cents in stamps. Some authors with a first contract consult a lawyer. Or you might find a literary agent whom you consult just this one time. The agent will charge you for the time spent—ask about this in advance—but on the advice of that agent you might ask to have certain paragraphs in the contract crossed out. The publisher may not agree to the change, and as a beginner eager to get your first book into print you should not insist. It will give you a good feeling to have a signed contract tucked away and to pretty well understand the details of the agreement you have entered upon. If there are some clauses you do not much care for, well, there will be other contracts and you will gain clout as you gain experience and importance.

## Should You Take the Advance?

Your contract will offer an advance payment. Advances vary from a few hundred dollars to many thousands, depending on the publisher and on the importance of the author or the book. A small, fairly new publisher with little money to play with might even ask you to forego any advance, and if you are eager to get your first book into print and the contract is acceptable except for that detail, you would be wise to agree. But whatever advance is offered, take it; it will be money in the bank drawing interest. Once your manuscript has been definitely accepted by the publisher the advance money is yours. If the book never earns that amount, the publisher takes the loss.

## What Is a Subsidiary Sale?

A subsidiary sale is any offshoot of the original sale: a sale of your book by the publisher for a paperback or special edition, a junior book club, translation and publication in a foreign country, an anthology, school textbook and teachers' manual. A TV use is a subsidiary sale. Your contract will state what percentage of the profits of a subsidiary sale will come to you.

The publisher should (but does not always) notify you whenever a subsidiary sale is made, state the terms of the sale, and tell you when the subsidiary publication will appear. You should be informed as to what percentage of the proceeds belong to you and will be included at the proper time in your royalty statement and check.

Subsidiary sales are profitable, and they can expand and extend the life of your book. Such sales may be made after the original edition has gone out of print because sales have fallen off.

If someone seeking a subsidiary right mistakenly applies to you for permission, forward the request to your publisher immediately. Take no action yourself.

# What About Royalties?

The usual rate of royalty on juvenile books is ten percent of the retail price, on a picture book five percent each for author and artist. There may possibly be an escalator clause—a provision for the publisher to pay you a higher royalty when sales reach a given figure.

The Authors Guild wants juvenile authors to try and get as high a royalty as adult authors receive, but if you ask for more your editor may tell you flatly that is all they can afford to pay. I recommend that at the start of your career you accept the royalty figure without argument. The royalty rate on paperbacks is much lower, but at least theoretically many more copies will be sold.

Royalties, with a statement of how many copies of your book have been sold and any subsidiary sales, are paid at stated times, sometimes twice a year, sometimes once a year, and there is always a time lag for bookkeeping purposes. If you receive royalties in May, the money will cover sales between the preceding June and December. Find the place in the contract that states when royalties are paid, so you will know when to expect the check. Patience is in order; the check probably will not arrive on the day it is due.

Keep in mind the contract provisions concerning your share of monies from subsidiary rights sales. There can be perfectly honest errors that no one will catch but you. Once my publisher deducted from my royalties an advance payment that I had never asked for or received. Another time they paid me half of the fee for a TV use instead of seventy-five percent, and my eagle eye spotted that.

And once a TV company informed the IRS that it had paid me quite a large sum. I had never received that money, didn't know what it was for. I wrote to inquire and learned that the payment was for the Saturday morning serial *The Puppy's Great Adventures,* which was based on *The Puppy Who Wanted a Boy*. A call to my editor found the publisher, too, drawing a blank. The subsidiary rights manager found the money, which had rightly been sent to them instead of to me, and my share came with my next royalty statement. That episode took a bit of clearing up with the IRS.

It is proper to be watchful of your rights, but don't be suspicious. Don't take the attitude that your publisher will cheat you if possible. I have been impressed by the honesty of publishers—even if some do slip in nasty clauses. Often one of my magazine stories or part of a book could have been used in a school reader or anthology and I never would have known. I was always informed, with payment forthcoming. Other authors may tell a different story; I can only tell you what my experience has been through forty-five years of writing and selling books.

## How Much Money Will You Make?

What you will earn from a book depends on how many copies are sold, the sale price of the book, how long the book stays in print, and subsidiary uses.

Suppose that in the first year 2,500 copies are sold and the book sells for $15. The total intake would be $37,500 and your ten percent would be $3,750, half of that for a picture book. From this your advance payment will be subtracted. As long as your book keeps on selling you will continue to receive royalties. The sales of the average book drop off considerably after the first year. But there is always the possibility of those subsidiary sales, including paperback rights and book clubs, and such sales may go on for years. The more books you write and the more you have in print, the better your royalties. As the retail prices of books increase, and they've been escalating steadily, your ten percent will increase too.

## What Should You Know About Copyright?

Copyright is protection of your work, under United States law, against any unauthorized use. Copyright law was revised in 1978 and the Copyright Office states: "No publication or registration or other action in the Copyright Office is required to secure copyright . . . There are, however, certain definite advantages to registration." You may not understand this, but your publisher does and will handle the details of copyright. A copyright notice must appear in every published book and your publisher must send a copy of your copyrighted book to the Library of Congress. Copyright covers your book for your lifetime plus fifty years.

One point should be made clear to authors and to the general public. I once saw a woman copying an entire book on a library copier and I made bold to ask if she knew she shouldn't do that. She said it was all right, the book was out of print. It was not all right. An out-of-print book is still protected for the term of the copyright. The publisher may decide to bring it back into print or another authorized user may do so.

You should have a general knowledge of copyright law. Send to the Copyright Office for the leaflet *Copyright Basics* and keep it in your file.

## What About Writing for Magazines?

You may already have sold little stories to some of the juvenile magazines that are listed in a market guide. This is a good thing to do. It gets your work into print and gives you excellent practice in writing. Some of the early stories I sold to magazines had to be so brief that I learned how to say a lot in tight space.

When my papers went into a university archive some years ago I found in my files an enormous thick folder recording the history of my writing for one religious publishing company. I do not belong to that sect; the stories were not religious. I suppose I found the name and sent them a story, and the history of that relationship is remarkable. I had forgotten the countless long letters I wrote, the detailed replies describing their needs. Perhaps they wanted a series of stories on animal homes, each a hundred words. The checks too were tiny, maybe two dollars or five dollars, but even those checks were welcome. I had given up my job as a copywriter and was earning a living by hook and by crook, the major crook writing.

Several magazine stories later became books. A number of stories were collected in a read-aloud volume that sold on racks. Some magazine stories too fragile to become books may be used over and over for years, perhaps in a school reader and teachers' manual that keeps being revised. You will be applied to at the proper time and you will be paid for each use.

When you sell to a magazine there is one important detail to watch: Be sure you are selling first serial rights only, which means just that one use. If the magazine tells you its policy is to buy all rights, ask if it will assign all other rights to you after publication. If not, don't sell, however tempting. Once your story has achieved exposure in a magazine you may receive requests to use it in an anthology or school reader. You may sell it later as a picture book.

Another detail: Should you sell a story to both a magazine and a book publisher at about the same time, tell the magazine editor your story must be published before the book comes out. Otherwise copyright will be affected.

## What About Taxes on Royalties?

You must pay taxes on your writing income as you do on any income. The tax laws applying to authors change, so you will need to get information at tax time from a tax accountant as to what extent you may deduct expenses you incurred in writing your book.

## Are There Organizations for Authors?

The official voice of authors is the Authors Guild, an arm of the Authors League of America. The Guild has done and continues to do yeoman's service in the interest of authors' rights, better contracts and fairer taxes. It offers reference material on contracts, copyright, and taxes. *The Authors Guild Bulletin* is informative and interesting. You might wait to join, however, until you begin to feel established.

The Society of Children's Book Writers you should join. This organization, with a membership of four thousand, is open to all, published or unpublished, who have an interest in children's literature. Your dues of thirty-five dollars a year will be well spent. The Society will send you a bi-monthly bulletin with information on markets and news of publishing. Of special value to you are the names of publishing houses on the lookout for new writers. The Society has leaflets on contracts, copyright, and agents; it offers grants and sponsors meetings and workshops.

These organizations' addresses will be found in the Appendix.

## Will a Course or a Conference Help?

A course in juvenile writing started me on my writing career by teaching me techniques. I had unconsciously been employing techniques in my little magazine stories, but how to put a book together was a bafflement. You, I hope, are learning about techniques from this present volume, but if you take a course you will have your work discussed and criticized. Many universities offer a course in writing for children.

Before you sign up for a correspondence course in writing inquire into the credentials of the people offering and teaching the course. And swallow with that grain of salt avowals that you will surely become a successful author if you take the course.

There are many conferences about juvenile writing, and here I am of two minds. You will find a conference of interest, you will hear from published authors and take copious notes. The question is whether you would be better off at home, writing, revising, polishing your own work, not in total ignorance of writing techniques but in the light of some understanding of how to go about it. That light will grow brighter as you practice and improve and exercise all the muscles of your imagination and brain power. The creative process itself, not listening to how someone else has done it, will turn you into a finished writer.

## Should You Subscribe to a Clipping Service?

When your first book is published you will receive offers to send you newspaper and magazine reviews of your work, at a price. You do not need a clipping service. Your publisher is even more interested in reviews than you are and will keep track and send you copies.

## Should You Keep Records?

It is important to keep records of correspondence, royalties, subsidiary sales, reviews—everything pertaining to a book. You may or may not keep—I have not—early and later revised versions of a work, as a matter of possible interest to researchers when you have become famous. Have a separate file folder for each book. You will also need a folder with your publisher's name on it, for correspondence not relating to one particular book.

When a new editor was considering my eighty-eighth book she asked for sales figures on the earlier books about Gus, my ghost, and reviews, to check on my track record. I had that information.

In the case of magazine stories, keep a copy of the story and be sure it bears the name of the magazine, date of publication, and date of copyright, which you will find in the front of the magazine. One copyright usually covers the entire contents of an issue.

When some of my magazine stories were gathered into a book I faced the horrendous task of tracking down twenty-six copyrights. Some of the magazines had gone out of existence. In a few cases I had to resort to a search by the Copyright Office. A copyright search involves a fee but it produces results. The record is there somewhere and can be found.

These are the bare bones of information you should have as you embark on your writing career.

# Epilogue

I have probably impressed and depressed you by all the drudgery, slavery, and business considerations. I've stressed the excruciating effort by which ideas are extracted from the depths of the mind and set down on paper in a form, you are aware, that does not match the perfection of their conception. I have tried to give you an honest picture of the disappointments in an author's life.

There is another dark side. A publishing house, which is in business to earn money, cannot afford to keep books in print when sales dwindle. Paperback publication saves many a book from extinction.

If you are a true writer you will be so involved with your next book that any bad news from your publisher, while not cheery, will not bow you down for long. Your editor will be looking for that next book. The more books you write for a publisher the more valuable you become as an income-producing property.

I have driven all this home to make sure you know what you are getting into when you begin to write.

Now comes the best part—the joys of writing!

There is the exhilaration of writing when you love what you are writing. You are creating a little world between the covers of a book. You are a sculptor, chipping away all that doesn't belong in that story-world. Rewriting can be satisfying because you are coming closer to your goal. Typing that final clean copy can soothe.

There is delight in working with words because if you are a writer you love the magic of words and you love using words to bring children into the world you are creating. There is the joy of sharing a place, a joke, a beauty, a secret with children who will laugh and cry and read on and write you little letters that say, "You are my favorite author."

When you are deeply involved in a writing project the adrenaline will flow, stimulating you to more work, in addition to other chores and responsibilities, than you dreamed you could accomplish.

There is the satisfaction of the letter or phone call to say an editor likes what you have written, even when revision lies ahead; the absorption of doing that revision, knowing now more clearly where you are heading. The final acceptance. The contract. The finished book in your hands.

Then the reviews, the adulation of friends, the public reaction to your excellence as a writer. There will be poor reviews too, but you learn to take them in stride. The readers, not the critics, decide.

Maybe a junior book club adopts your book. And finally the check. Even if writing is a secondary source of income, as it is for most authors, the check is important.

You will be asked to speak to children in schools and they will sit on the floor and gaze up at you and ask you where you get your ideas and how long it takes to write a book and how much money you make—and other questions you learn to expect. You will go away enlivened, and those faces will give new meaning to your work as you return to your typewriter.

Of one thing I warn you: Most children's authors are famous to no one but librarians and teachers and the children who write to you or hear you speak. Children often know the title of a book they love but not the name of the author. You will not be famous to the general public except sometimes in your hometown. Pay it no mind. Be amused.

# The Story of a Story

I told you earlier that even one good little story is worth doing. To prove that one little story can live on, I shall tell you about *The Puppy Who Wanted a Boy*.

In 1946 I wrote that story and sold it to a magazine, *Story Parade*. They paid me fifteen dollars. Almost at once came requests for other uses. The story was sold, with half the fees coming to me, to the Southern Baptist Convention, *University Society Anthology, Children's Digest, Holiday Story Book,* a children's magazine in Sweden, *Santa Claus Book, Treat Shop, Children's Hour, Tall Book of Christmas*. It was read on radio story hours and translated into braille. A manufacturer featured *Puppy* in its Christmas house organ and sent me one of its products, an automatic timer that turned on my light for years.

Meanwhile I was trying to sell the story as a book. Several publishers turned it down. Then Lee Kingman at Houghton Mifflin said she would buy the story were she not leaving that publisher. If I wanted to get it into print, she said, and would accept a flat fee instead of a royalty, try the Dennison Manufacturing Company, which was starting a low-cost project. I sold the story to Dennison for two hundred and fifty dollars—all rights. I would receive no more money, ever, for that book.

The Dennison project lagged, and one day Lockie Parker, editor of *Story Parade,* called me. "See if you can buy that story back," she said. "Grosset and Dunlap would like it.'

After haggling, I did buy it back, for a hundred and twenty-five dollars, and sold it to Grosset and Dunlap for two hundred and fifty—again all rights forever. And once more the project couldn't get off the ground. I bought the story back again.

By this time William Morrow and Company had published a number of my books, and one day at lunch I said to my editor, Elisabeth Hamilton, "You would never be so foolish, would you, as to make a book of a story that has had all this exposure?" "We might," she said.

They did, in 1959. *Weekly Reader* took the book the next year for its book club. Scott Foresman did a reprint edition. In 1970 Morrow brought out a Spanish edition, mostly for New York City. *Puppy* became a TV cartoon series that ran for two years.

Spurred to action by the TV *Puppy,* Morrow brought out a new edition with a new puppy in 1985. In 1988 *Puppy* appeared in paperback and became a "Reading Rainbow Book," recommended by a juvenile TV program. Again *Weekly Reader* offered the book to its members.

Only my guardian angel twice saved me from consequences of a hideous mistake. This history is to pound home my point: Never, never sell all rights to a story for one flat fee. Two generations of children have loved the book. I've had forty-plus years of profits. The book may go on now for another forty years.

The other lesson is: Never regard any story, however simple, as unimportant. Every story is worthy of the best creative effort you can possibly bring to it.

I remember so well when my first chapter-book was accepted. I had made all the changes the editor had suggested and returned the manuscript to her. Often I had dreamed of a telephone call saying my book had been accepted, but when the call actually came I couldn't believe it. Either she thought she was talking to someone else or my ears were playing me tricks. Then the contract came. I walked up Fifth Avenue feeling, I am sure, the way a woman feels when she knows, and no one else knows, she is going to have a baby.

This volume is about having a book. I hope it will help.

# Appendix

## 1. Resources

### *Some Books That Will Help*

*A Critical History of Children's Literature* by Cornelia Meigs, Elizabeth Nesbitt, Anne Eaton, Ruth Hall Viguers. Macmillan, New York, 1953. Out of print.

*The Unreluctant Years, a Critical Approach to Children's Literature* by Lillian H. Smith. American Library Assn., Chicago, 1953. Out of print.

A good dictionary such as *The Random House Dictionary of the English Language, Second Edition, Unabridged.* Random House, New York.
or
*Webster's Third New International Dictionary, Unabridged.* Merriam-Webster, Springfield, MA
or
*Funk & Wagnalls Standard Dictionary*. New American Library (Signet), New York, 1980.

A world atlas, such as *The New International Atlas,* Rand McNally, Chicago.

*The Encyclopedia Britannica*

*Books in Print*

*Who's Who in America*

*Literary Marketplace*

*The Elements of Style* by William Strunk, Jr., and E. B. White. Macmillan, New York, 1979. Paperback only.

The above reference books should be found in your public library. The Strunk and White book you should own.

## Some Addresses

The Authors Guild, Inc.
234 West 44th Street
New York, NY 10036

Society of Children's Book Writers
P.O. Box 296, Mar Vista Station
Los Angeles, CA 90066

Copyright Office
Library of Congress
Washington, DC 20559
Telephone: 202-479-0700

# 2. Books Cited or Quoted

Look in your library's file catalogue, under title or author, for these books. If the ones you wish to read are not there ask to have them borrowed from another library. Some are out of print; most should be obtainable. I wish to thank the authors whose books are cited or quoted.

Armstrong, William H., *Sounder.* Harper and Row, New York, 1969. Also paperback.

Aaseng, Nathan, *Pete Rose.* Lerner Publications Co., Minneapolis, 1981.

Austen, Jane, *Pride and Prejudice.* Raintree, New York, 1981. Also paperback.

Babbitt, Natalie, *The Search for Delicious.* Farrar, Straus and Giroux, New York, 1969.

———, *Tuck Everlasting.* Farrar, Straus and Giroux, New York, 1975. Also paperback.

Baum, L. Frank, *The Wonderful Wizard of Oz.* William Morrow and Co., New York, 1987. Also paperback.

Beatty, Patricia, *Jonathan Down Under.* William Morrow and Co., New York, 1982. Also paperback.

———, *Turn Homeward, Hannalee.* William Morrow and Co., New York, 1984. Also paperback.

Blume, Judy, *Then Again Maybe I Won't.* Bradbury Press, New York, 1971. Also paperback.

Busch, Phyllis S. *Cactus in the Desert.* T. Y. Crowell, New York, 1979. Also paperback.

Byars, Betsy, *Cracker Jackson.* Viking, New York, 1985. Also paperback.

———, *The Pinballs.* Harper and Row, New York, 1977. Also paperback.

Canfield, Dorothy, *Understood Betsy.* Buccaneer Books, Cutchogue, NY, 1981. Also paperback.

Carroll, Lewis, *Alice's Adventures in Wonderland.* Putnam Publishing Group, New York, 1981. Also paperback.

Cone, Molly, *The Amazing Memory of Harvey Bean.* Houghton Mifflin Co., Boston, 1980.

Corbett, Scott, *The Case of the Silver Skull.* Little Brown and Co., Inc., Boston, 1974.

Cormier, Robert, *The Chocolate War.* Pantheon Books, Inc., New York, 1974. Also paperback.

Danziger, Paula, *The Divorce Express.* Delacorte Press, New York, 1982. Also paperback.

Davies, Robertson, *A Mixture of Frailties.* Penguin Books, New York, 1980. Paperback only.

de Angeli, Marguerite, *The Door in the Wall.* Scholastic, Inc., New York, 1984. Paperback only.

Fitzhugh, Louise, *Harriet the Spy.* Harper and Row, New York, 1978. Also paperback.

Fox, Paula, *Lily and the Lost Boy.* Franklin Watts, Inc., New York, 1987. Also paperback.

Fritz, Jean, *And Then What Happened, Paul Revere?* Putnam Publishing Group, 1973. Also paperback.

———,*Homesick: My Own Story.* Putnam Publishing Group, New York, 1982. Also paperback.

George, Jean Craighead, *Julie of the Wolves.* Harper and Row, New York, 1972. Also paperback.

Hamilton, Virginia, *Sweet Whispers, Brother Rush.* Putnam Publishing Group, New York, 1982. Also paperback.

Henry, Marguerite, *King of the Wind*. Macmillan Publishing Co., New York, 1948. Also paperback.
———, *Misty of Chincoteaque*. Rand McNally, Chicago, Illinois.
Hunter, Mollie, *The Wicked One*. Harper and Row, New York, 1977. Also paperback.
Jablonski, Edward, *Gershwin: a Biography*. Doubleday and Co., New York, 1987. Paperback only.
Keats, Ezra Jack, *John Henry: an American Legend*. Alfred A. Knopf, Inc., New York, 1987. Also paperback.
Lee, Harper, *To Kill a Mocking Bird*. Harper and Row, New York, 1961. Also paperback.
Lewis, C. S., *The Magician's Nephew*. Macmillan Publishing Co., New York, 1969. Also paperback.
———, *The Lion, the Witch and the Wardrobe*. Macmillan Publishing Co., New York, 1968. Also paperback.
Lobel, Arnold, *Frog and Toad Are Friends*. Harper and Row, New York, 1973. Also paperback.
Locker, Thomas (book listed under Lenny Hort), *The Boy Who Held Back the Sea*. Dial Books, New York, 1987.
London, Jack, *The Call of the Wild*. Macmillan Publishing Co., New York, 1970. Also paperback.
MacLachlan, Patricia, *Sarah, Plain and Tall*. Harper and Row, New York, 1985. Also paperback.
Mazer, Harry, *The Last Mission*. Dell Publishing Co., New York, 1981. Paperback only.
McCloskey, Robert, *Make Way for Ducklings*. Viking, New York, 1941. Also paperback.
Meigs, Cornelia, *Invincible Louisa*. Little Brown and Co., Inc., Boston, 1969. Also paperback.
Montgomery, L. M., *Anne of Green Gables*. Putnam Publishing Group, New York, 1983. Also paperback.
Musgrove, Margaret, illustrated by Leon and Diane Dillion, *Ashanti to Zulu: African Traditions*. Dial Books, New York, 1980. Also paperback.
Neville, Emily, *It's Like This, Cat*. Harper and Row, New York, 1963. Also paperback.
Parry, Marian, illustrator of fable, *City Mouse, Country Mouse*. Scholastic, Inc., New York, 1971. Paperback only.
Paterson, Katherine, *Bridge to Terabithia*. T. Y. Crowell, New York, 1977. Also paperback.
Paterson, Katherine, *The Great Gilly Hopkins*. T. Y. Crowell, New York, 1978. Also paperback.

Paterson, Katherine, *Jacob Have I Loved.* T. Y. Crowell, New York, 1980. Also paperback.

Potter, Beatrix, *The Tailor of Gloucester.* Frederick Warne, New York, 1968. Also paperback.

Provenson, Alice and Martin, *The Glorious Flight Across the Channel with Louis Bleriot.* Viking, New York, 1983. Also paperback.

Rawls, Wilson, *Where the Red Fern Grows.* Doubleday and Co., New York, 1973. Also paperback.

Simon, Norma, *Why Am I Different?* Albert Whitman, Niles, IL, 1976.

Spyri, Johanna, *Heidi.* Julian Messner and Co., New York, 1981. Also paperback.

Thayer, Jane, *Gus Loved His Happy Home.* The Shoe String Press, Hamden, CT, 1989.

———, *The Popcorn Dragon.* William Morrow and Co., New York, 1989.

———, *The Puppy Who Wanted a Boy.* William Morrow and Co., New York, 1988. Also paperback.

———, *Quiet on Account of Dinosaur,* William Morrow and Co., New York, 1988. Also paperback.

Travers, Pamela L., *Mary Poppins.* Buccaneer Books, Cutchogue, NY, 1981. Also paperback.

Tresselt, Alvin, *Hide and Seek Fog.* Lothrop, Lee and Shepard, New York, 1968. Also paperback.

———, *White Snow, Bright Snow.* William Morrow and Co., New York, date not set. Paperback.

Van Allsburg, Chris, *The Polar Express.* Houghton Mifflin Co., Boston, 1985.

Voigt, Cynthia, *Dicey's Song.* Macmillan Publishing Co., New York, 1982.

———, *A Solitary Blue.* Macmillan Publishing Co., New York, 1983.

Watkins, Yoko Kawashima, *So Far From the Bamboo Grove.* Lothrop Lee and Shepard, New York, 1986. Also paperback.

Watson, Clyde, *Tom Fox and the Apple Pie.* T. Y. Crowell, New York, 1972.

Watson, Nancy Dingman, *The Birthday Goat.* T. Y. Crowell, New York, 1974.

White, E. B., *Charlotte's Web.* Harper and Row, New York, 1952. Also paperback.

Wilder, Laura Ingalls, *The Little House in the Big Woods.* Harper and Row, New York, 1953. Also paperback.

Woolley, Catherine, *Cathy Leonard Calling.* Viking Penguin, New York, 1988. Paperback only.

———, *Ginnie and Geneva.* Viking Penguin, New York, 1988. Paperback only.

Yolen, Jane, *Owl Moon.* Putnam Publishing Group, New York, 1987.

The following books are not listed in the 1988–89 BOOKS IN PRINT, so they may be considered out of print. Some are still on library shelves and can be borrowed if not available in your library. Also, books are constantly coming back into print in paperback.

Baum, L. Frank, *The Sea Fairies.* Reilly and Britton, Chicago, 1911.

Brown, Margaret Wise, *The Country Noisy Book.* Harper and Row, New York, 1940.

Cavanna, Betty, *Mystery on Safari.* William Morrow and Co., New York, 1970.

Corcoran, Barbara, *Me and You and a Dog Named Blue.* Atheneum, New York, 1979.

de Angeli, Marguerite, *Thee, Hannah.* Doubleday, New York, 1940.

Paterson, Katherine, *Sing, Jimmy Jo.* E. P. Dutton, New York. 1985.

Sharmat, Marjorie, *The Lancelot Closes at Five.* Macmillan, New York, 1979.

Thayer, Jane: *Andy Wouldn't Talk; The Blueberry Pie Elf; The Cat That Joined the Club; Curious, Furious Chipmunk; Emerald Enjoyed the Moonlight; Gus Was a Friendly Ghost; Mr. Turtle's Magic Glasses: The Mouse on the Fourteenth Floor; The Outside Cat; Rockets Don't Go to Chicago, Andy; Try Your Hand; Where's Andy?; Andy and Mr. Cunningham; The Pussy Who Went to the Moon;* and *Where Is Squirrel?* William Morrow & Co., New York.

Watson, Nancy Dingman, *Blueberries Lavender.* Addison Wesley, Reading, MA, 1977.

———, *Marcus Agruncus, a Bad Little Mouse.* Western Publishing Co., Racine, WI, 1976.

———, *New Under the Stars*. Little Brown, Boston, 1970.

White, E. B., *Letters of E. B. White*, Collected and edited by Dorothy Lobrano, New York, 1976.

Wolfe, Virginia, *To the Lighthouse*. Harcourt Brace Jovanovich, New York, 1927.

Woolley, Catherine: *Cathy and the Beautiful People; Cathy Uncovers a Secret, David's Campaign Buttons; Ginnie and Geneva Cookbook; Ginnie and Her Juniors; Ginnie and the Mystery Doll; Ginnie and the Mystery House; Ginnie and the Mystery Light; Ginnie Joins In; Libby Shadows a Lady; Libby's Uninvited Guest; Look Alive Libby; A Room for Cathy*. William Morrow & Co., New York.

# Index